FREE online study and revision support available at **www.oup.com/lawrevision**

Take your learning further with:

- Multiple-choice questions with instant feedback
- Interactive glossaries and flashcards of key cases
- Tips, tricks and audio advice
- Annotated outline answers
- Diagnostic tests show you where to concentrate
- Extra questions, key facts checklists, and topic overviews

unique features

student-focused online support

Acknowledgements

Dedicated to Isabelle, Mia, and Lydia May.

We would like to express our gratitude to our publishers for all their help and encouragement in the preparation of this fourth edition. We also gratefully acknowledge the help and advice provided through the comments sourced from the anonymous expert reviewers. Finally, we would like to specifically express our gratitude and sincere thanks to Hannah Wright. Hannah sourced expert reviews which have identified areas for improvements and greater focus, and has shared with us her enthusiasm and comments for the development of the new edition.

James Marson and Katy Ferris
Sheffield, January 2019

New to this edition

- Recent case law discussing the potential implications of Brexit (*Case C-621/18 Wightman and Others v Secretary of State for Exiting the European Union* [2018]). This updated edition includes important cases in contract law including *Goodlife Foods Ltd v Hall Fire Protection Ltd* [2018] on the reasonableness test in UCTA 1977; *Morris-Garner v One Step (Support) Ltd* [2018] where the Supreme Court reaffirmed the compensatory nature of damages; *MSC Mediterranean Shipping Company S.A. v Cottonex Anstalt* [2016] on affirming a contract where no legitimate interest exists; *Rock Advertising Ltd v MWB Business Exchange Centres Ltd* [2018] on no oral modification clauses and consideration in contracts; and *Wood v Capita Insurance Services Limited* [2017] on the interpretation of contractual terms. In torts law, *Jackson v Murray & another* [2015] is included given its implications for appeal courts' interference with findings of fact by the court at first instance and *Lejonvarn v Burgess & Anor* [2017] offers instruction as to the imposition of a legal duty of care where advice is given by a professional in a social context. Employment law has been subject to several changes, including the removal of fees for cases of dismissals to employment tribunals. The Supreme Court has provided instruction as to the distinction between workers and independent contractors in *Pimlico Plumbers & Charlie Mullins v Gary Smith* [2018], and it determined direct discrimination in the Christian baker case (*Lee v Ashers Baking Company Ltd* [2018]). *Gray v Mulberry* [2018] is also included on the potential for protection against discrimination on the basis of a philosophical belief (the sanctity of copyright law). The Court of Justice of the European Union has instructed national courts on the application of dress codes in relation to the manifestation of political, philosophical, and religious beliefs (*Case C-157/15 Achbita,*

Centrum voor Gelijkheid van kansen en voor racismebestrijding v G4S Secure Solutions
[2017]). The Court of Appeal has determined where inaction can amount to gross misconduct in *Adesokan v Sainsbury's Supermarkets Ltd* [2017]. The Employment Appeal
Tribunal has also been active on the rights of employees to receive a statement of written
particulars before the two-month statutory deadline (*Stefanko and others v Maritime
Hotel Ltd* [2018]). In intellectual property law, the Court of Justice has also determined
the possibility to copyright protection food in *Case C-310/17 Levola Hengelo BV v Smilde
Foods BV* [2018].

• Recent legislation and its effects in these jurisdictions of law include the Data Protection
Act 2018; the Data Protection Directive (95/46/EC); The Employment Rights (Employment
Particulars and Paid Annual Leave) (Amendment) Regulations 2018; The Employment Rights (Miscellaneous Amendments) Regulations 2019; the Equality Act 2010
(Gender Pay Gap Information) Regulations 2017; the Equality Act 2010 (Specific Duties
and Public Authorities) Regulations 2017; the General Data Protection Regulation ((EU)
2016/679); The Finance Bill 2017; the Intellectual Property (Unjustified Threats) Act 2017;
the Law Enforcement Directive; and the Parental Bereavement (Leave and Pay) Act 2018.

Business Law
Concentrate

4th edition

James Marson

Reader in Law
Sheffield Hallam University

Katy Ferris

Assistant Professor in Business Law
Nottingham University Business School

OXFORD
UNIVERSITY PRESS

OXFORD

UNIVERSITY PRESS

Great Clarendon Street, Oxford, OX2 6DP,
United Kingdom

Oxford University Press is a department of the University of Oxford.
It furthers the University's objective of excellence in research, scholarship,
and education by publishing worldwide. Oxford is a registered trade mark of
Oxford University Press in the UK and in certain other countries

First edition 2010
Second edition 2013
Third edition 2016

Impression: 1

Public sector information reproduced under Open Government Licence v3.0
(http://www.nationalarchives.gov.uk/doc/open-government-licence/open-government-licence.htm)

Published in the United States of America by Oxford University Press
198 Madison Avenue, New York, NY 10016, United States of America

British Library Cataloguing in Publication Data
Data available

Library of Congress Control Number: 2019936395

ISBN 978-0-19-884060-2

Printed in Great Britain by
Ashford Colour Press Ltd, Gosport, Hampshire

Contents

Table of cases

Table of cases

✳✳✳✳✳✳✳✳✳✳✳✳

Table of cases

****

Table of legislation

Table of legislation

****

Table of legislation

****

Table of secondary legislation

#1

The English legal system

Key facts

- Depending on the legal dispute, a claim may be heard in any number of courts and it is necessary to know of their jurisdiction and their 'importance' in relation to the hierarchical system affecting precedent.

- In precedent, it is necessary to distinguish between the *ratio decidendi* and *obiter dicta* in judgments.

- The United Kingdom's membership of the European Union (EU) has significantly affected the constitution and jurisdictions of law including contract, employment, and company laws. You must be aware of the influence membership of the EU has on 'domestic' laws.

- The **Human Rights Act (HRA) 1998** has an impact on businesses in both the private and public sectors. Its scope and application must be appreciated to ensure compliance with the law.

- It is imperative to note that whilst the traditional court system is appropriate to resolve some disputes, it should not be considered as the only, or indeed the primary, forum. Alternative forms of dispute resolution may be more suitable and conducive to continuing business relationships and should be explored in the first instance.

Introduction

Questions on the English Legal System typically take an essay form rather than problem scenarios. Such questions may require you to critique the development of the **common law**, the question could relate to the role of the **judiciary** in interpreting **legislation**, you may be asked to consider the impact of the **HRA 1998** on the **constitution**, or a question may involve the implications of the UK's membership of the EU. When faced with essay questions in these areas, it is important to adopt a critical/analytical approach (identify and explain both sides of the argument). Include relevant common law and/or statutory examples to 'ground' your arguments.

While problem-type questions in this area are not common, the use of Alternative Dispute Resolution (ADR) in business scenarios would be a typical example and one is used at the end of this chapter. Such a problem question requires an understanding of the various forms of ADR and a discussion of its use to resolve business problems, along with its limitations compared with the traditional court system.

Revision Tip

Always use case law/statutory materials in an answer. Whilst not lawyers, this is a law module hence your answers must contain reference to appropriate legal materials! Case law should concern the *ratio* rather than a lengthy recitation of the facts. Identify the question you are being asked and the jurisdiction of law applicable, describe that law, and then apply the law and/or provide your critical analysis. This will ensure you maximize your marks and enable you to offer a full answer.

Criminal and civil law

Generally, criminal law regulates activities which the law has prohibited. Business activities can involve both criminal and civil liability.

Civil law is of most significance in business law as it regulates actions between parties, for example in agreements they have voluntarily entered or where society has placed an obligation to take reasonable care not to cause damage or injury to others. Civil cases involve a system of remedies. Civil cases are determined on the 'balance of probabilities' whilst the burden on the State in (most) criminal cases is to establish guilt 'beyond reasonable doubt'.

An overview of the courts

The jurisdiction of the courts is provided through **Parliament**. Some courts may hear both civil and criminal cases under their jurisdiction (such as the Court of Appeal and the Supreme Court, although there is a clear demarcation between the two jurisdictions). The courts also exist under a hierarchical system where a decision of the higher court is binding as a **precedent** on those courts below it.

Figure 1.1 Hierarchy of the courts

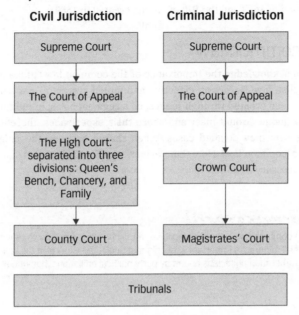

Tribunals are established with jurisdiction for specific areas of law. Tribunals do not establish precedent and hence, particularly in employment tribunals, this leads to inconsistent awards. As such, predicting or 'second-guessing', decisions is almost impossible.

Precedent follows the direction of the arrows in Fig 1.1.

Revision Tip

The magistrates' court plays a key role in the administration of the criminal justice system, but note that it also hears civil cases. Examples of the civil element include licensing, betting and gaming, civil debts, and so on.

Sources of law

Revision Tip

Every law that is mentioned in lectures, books, and so on has a source of **statute**, common law, equity, custom, convention, or law from the EU. You are undertaking assessment in a law module therefore you will be heavily penalized if you do not cite the 'law' that gives authority for your arguments.

The sources must be viewed as a system as a whole, each with a positive and important role to play in defining the laws of the UK. Some of these sources are more significant and relevant than others, but it is important to recognize statutes as the highest form of law (consider the Glorious Revolution of 1688 and the **Bill of Rights** created in 1689).

Case law/common law

It is necessary to acknowledge the importance of the common law (judge-made law) in the formation of English law. Before an effective and united system of government existed in the UK, laws had been created through judges, on a regional basis, in judging cases brought before them. The judges would meet and share their experiences, thereby explaining the rationale for the way they decided cases. When shared between the judges, this started the formation of a 'common law'. Note that Parliament will only legislate against the common law where it is necessary to do so.

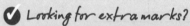 *Looking for extra marks?*

Advantages of the common law include its flexibility. It may be altered quickly to reflect changes in public policy/societal factors. An important aspect is that unelected experts in the law (judges) make the common law rather than politicians bound by party political affiliations (but who are publicly accountable).

Precedent

The hierarchy of the courts not only reflects the seniority of the members of the judiciary who hear the cases, but it also affects the power of the principles of law established to bind the lower courts. Precedent is based on the doctrine of **stare decisis** (which means 'stand by what has been previously decided'). However, judges in lower courts may deviate from an established precedent where there is a material difference between that case and the one being heard. This is known as 'distinguishing' a precedent. Higher courts also possess the power to 'reverse' a precedent.

Ratio decidendi and obiter dicta

The **ratio decidendi** is the 'reason for the decision' and involves a point of law rather than the facts of the case. The **ratio** is the precedent. Judges may also make pronouncements **obiter dicta** (something said by the way). As **obiter dicta** statements are not pertinent to the judgment provided in the case, they will not form a precedent, but may form a persuasive authority if a future case does come before the courts with a similar legal position.

Legislation

Legislation refers to laws passed through Parliament and may be called statutes and/or Acts of Parliament. Time constraints limit the ability of Parliament to pass all legislation that is needed and therefore that task is often delegated to some other body (but which is answerable to Parliament and must act in accordance with Parliament's instructions). Primary legislation is passed through Parliament and this involves matters of general national importance and significance, whereas **delegated legislation** is secondary legislation passed under the guidance of a government minister.

Statutory interpretation

Rules/approaches of interpreting legislation have been established to aid in consistency:

- The Literal Rule: this is a traditional (and possibly most 'pure') approach where the judges look to the text in the legislation and give it its plain and ordinary meaning. The **Interpretation Act 1978** enabled judges to seek use of definitions without being limited to, for example, the Oxford English Dictionary.

- The Golden Rule: here judges are provided with the option of interpreting ambiguous legislation in a way that would otherwise lead to an absurd result if its literal meaning were given (*Grey v Pearson* [1857]). It may also be used to prevent a result that would be contrary to public policy if a literal approach were adopted (*Re Sigsworth* [1935]).

- The Mischief Rule: this enables the judiciary to interpret legislation in light of the mischief/problem that the legislation had intended to remove (*Smith v Hughes* [1960]).

- The Purposive/Teleological Method: the courts in this jurisdiction have an obligation to follow the decisions of the Court of Justice of the European Union (CJEU) (when considering laws either emanating from the EU or with an EU dimension) and adopt a purposive approach to interpretation. This approach looks to the spirit or intent of the legislation, and to interpret it accordingly. A similar approach is adopted in the interpretation, and application, of the **HRA 1998** with the **European Convention on Human Rights (ECHR)**.

Revision tip

The power of a purposive form of statutory interpretation can be seen in the seminal case *Marleasing SA v La Comercial Internacional de Alimentación SA* [1991] where the CJEU permitted national courts to insert 'additional words . . . They could be taken out; they can be moved around' (at paragraph 49) to ensure domestic law conforms with the EU parent law. This power was extended in the case *Bernhard Pfeiffer et al v Deutsches Rotes Kreuz, Kreisverband Waldshut eV* [2004] where the obligation was imposed on courts and public bodies to give effect to superior EU laws. Remember these powers when discussing the implications on the UK's membership of the EU and the requirements on bodies to provide a consistent interpretation of EU law.

Equity

Equity provided the remedies of **injunctions, specific performance, rectification,** and **rescission,** whilst the common law only allowed claimants to pursue a damages action. The **Judicature Acts 1873 and 1875** provided that the available remedies established in equity and the common law could be provided by all courts (at their discretion).

Customs and conventions

Customs, as a source of law, are used increasingly sparingly in the modern era (eg the long-established rule that allowed fishermen to dry their nets on private land).

Conventions are usually historical ways, derived from established practices, in which individuals are required/expected to act. They are part of the uncodified constitution of the UK, and sometimes are (re)produced in written forms to 'formalize' the rule. Conventions are generally applicable to constitutional matters.

Delegated legislation

Delegated legislation refers to legislation that is passed by some individual/body other than Parliament. Parliament provides authority to the individual/body through an 'enabling' or 'parent' Act, and this establishes a framework of the law, and the powers and tasks to be undertaken in fulfilment of the parent Act.

The three forms of delegated legislation are:

- Statutory Instruments;
- Orders in Council (issued by the Privy Council);
- By-laws.

The European Union

Revision tip

Questions on EU law will generally be in essay-type form and focus on the way membership has impacted on the constitution, the powers held by Parliament, or how domestic laws have been altered through EU laws/decisions of the CJEU.

Membership of the EU

The UK became a signatory to the European Economic Community and the legislation that facilitated membership was the **European Communities Act (ECA) 1972**. Section 2(1) provides that EU law which is intended to take **direct effect** within Member States (eg the treaty Articles and Regulations—see Table 1.1) will automatically form part of the law in the UK and must be given such effect by the judiciary. The ECA 1972 instructs the judiciary to follow EU law even if it contradicts domestic law and if there is any doubt regarding the extent of the EU law or provision the matter should be referred to the CJEU for clarification (**Art 267 Treaty on the Functioning of the European Union (TFEU)**).

It will be remembered that on 29 March 2017 the UK notified the EU, through **Art 50 Treaty on European Union (TEU)** to withdraw its membership of the EU (triggering the UK's Brexit). This was due to take effect at 11pm (GMT) 29 March 2019. Given the problems

Table 1.1 Sources of law: Article 288 TFEU

	Primary law	Secondary laws		
	Treaty Articles	Regulations	Directives	Decisions
Directly effective	Yes (directly applicable)	Yes (directly applicable)	No	Yes (to whom they are addressed)
Horizontal direct effect	Yes	Yes	No	No
Vertical direct effect	Yes	Yes	Yes	Yes
Uniformity of laws	Yes	Yes	No (harmonization)	No

the government has experienced in obtaining agreement about the subsequent deal with the EU, and questions regarding whether the UK could reverse its notice to leave, the Court of Session referred such a question to the CJEU.

Case C-621/18 Wightman and Others v Secretary of State for Exiting the European Union [2018] ECLI:EU:C:2018:999

The Court declared that Art 50 TEU allows for the UK's unilateral revocation of its notification to withdraw from the EU. This has huge constitutional significance for the UK and any other Member State which uses Art 50 to notify the EU of its intention to leave, but later changes its decision. It does not require agreement from the other Member States (mutual consent) or the European Council to effectively reverse its decision to withdraw.

Interaction between domestic courts and the CJEU

One of the main features of the CJEU is its role in assisting domestic courts in the Member States to interpret, and thereby correctly apply, EU laws. The CJEU is a court of reference. The EU places obligations on Member States to follow the laws in the Treaties and those created by the Council, Commission, and Parliament (the most frequently used method, and most contentious, is Directives). Directives provide the Member State with discretion as to the method and form used to **transpose** the law. Member States often require assistance from the CJEU to interpret the meaning of the words used in the text of the law, and its extent. This mechanism ensures the harmonization of EU law between the Member States and a consistent approach to the application of the law.

The positioning of the CJEU in the legal system

The CJEU is not the highest court in England (a role occupied by the Supreme Court). As a court of reference, the CJEU provides an answer as to the scope/application of EU law in relation to the factual problem presented by the referring domestic court. The domestic court still issues the judgment, and the role played by the CJEU is in clarifying the contentious issue to ensure the referring court can provide a judgment in accordance with EU law.

Revision tip

The referring court must make sure the CJEU has not already answered the question presented under Art 267 TFEU in a previous case.

Constitutional impact on UK

The UK has an obligation to enforce and transpose EU laws, but also the judiciary is obliged to interpret laws consistently with EU law, even where the domestic law was effective before the EU law was enacted. This is where the reference procedure to the CJEU will come into effect. The CJEU's 'interpretative' function can lead to a change in the application of domestic law. In *Litster and Others v Forth Dry Dock & Engineering* [1990] this resulted in words being added to a statute to fulfil the UK's obligation to the EU.

Laws may be required to be altered to ensure conformity. In *Commission v UK* (Case 61/81) [1982] the UK had to amend the **Equal Pay Act 1970** to ensure that the provisions of the **Equal Pay Directive (Council Directive 75/117/EEC)** were correctly transposed. This required the inclusion of a 'third head' of complaint to ensure individuals had access to the protection that EU law provided.

In *Factortame* [1991] it was decided that an Act of Parliament that breached an EU Treaty Article had to be disapplied so as not to contravene a (superior) EU law.

Human rights

Whilst human rights can be broadly interpreted to include aspects of social rights, when spoken about in a legal context this is generally to refer to the **HRA 1998** and the **ECHR** (upon which the HRA is based). The UK has been a signatory to the **ECHR** since 1951 (its provisions coming into force in 1953), and incorporated these provisions through domestic legislation in 1998 (the **HRA 1998**, in force since 2 October 2000).

The European Convention on Human Rights

Remember that the ECHR is not part of the EU—they have different laws and are governed by different bodies, although States may be members of the EU and signatories to the ECHR.

Convention rights

The **ECHR**, and its subsequent extensions (protocols), ensured that the most significant civic and political rights were to be respected and protected by the signatory States to the Convention. They were to be enjoyed without discrimination (**Art 14**).

The most significant rights are shown in Table 1.2.

The **ECHR** allowed for enforcement of rights through the European Court of Human Rights (ECtHR) based in Strasbourg. For a claim to be admissible, it must have involved a point of law not already decided by the ECtHR (as domestic courts are already bound by precedents established in that court).

The Human Rights Act 1998

In 1998, the **HRA 1998** was enacted which meant that cases involving the **ECHR** could be heard by the UK courts and effective enforcement measures provided. The **HRA 1998** includes Arts 2–12 and 14 ECHR, Arts 1–3 of the First Protocol, and Arts 1 and 2 of the Sixth Protocol.

When enacting legislation, the **HRA 1998 s 19** places a responsibility on the relevant Minister presenting the Bill to make a statement regarding its compatibility with the Act, or otherwise to declare to Parliament that they are unable to offer such a statement, but the government wishes to proceed with the Bill regardless. This offers guidance to the judiciary in applying and interpreting the legislation.

Table 1.2 Key Convention rights

Article 2	The right to life
Article 3	Freedom from torture, inhumane and degrading punishment
Article 6	The right to fair trial
Article 9	Freedom of religion
Article 10	Freedom of expression
Article 11	Freedom of peaceful assembly
Article 12	The right to marry and found a family
Article 1 of the First Protocol	The right to an education
Article 3 of the First Protocol	The right to take part in free elections by secret ballot
The Sixth and Thirteenth Protocols	The abolition of the death penalty

Powers and responsibilities of the judiciary

Due to the **separation of powers**, and to ensure the judiciary were not granted powers reserved for constitutional/supreme courts, the authority provided to the judiciary had to be restricted when faced with a breach of human rights. When a breach is identified, the judiciary is not empowered to strike down the offending legislation. Precedent-making courts have the ability to issue a declaration of incompatibility with the ECHR (s 4(2)).

The HRA 1998 also imposes obligations on the judiciary when interpreting legislation. Section 2 HRA 1998 requires that courts and tribunals interpret domestic law consistently with previous decisions of the ECtHR where possible. 'Where possible' means that the judiciary is not empowered to change the wording of national legislation or alter its meaning simply to comply with the ECHR (*Ghaidan v Godin-Mendoza* [2004]).

Horizontal and vertical effect

The HRA 1998, and the ECHR that preceded it, places an obligation on the State, including public authorities (s 6), to act in accordance with the rights established in those documents. Direct challenges can be made against public authorities, including local and central government (vertical effect), and the common law is also subject to the Act.

The horizontal effect of the application of human rights refers to claims between private parties using the Articles of the ECHR. Historically this has proved to be difficult (see *Copsey v WWB Devon Clays Ltd* [2005]); however recent cases have demonstrated the effectiveness of human rights in dealings between private parties (*Eweida & Others v UK* [2013]).

> ✅ *Looking for extra marks?*
>
> Whilst use of the **ECHR** and its interpretative effect on the **HRA 1998** has proven to be limited in effectiveness when applied against a private person/body, recent case law has demonstrated a more enlightened approach by the judiciary. When addressing issues relating to the use between private parties of the **ECHR**, remember that much of the case law is fact-specific (so be careful of claiming that these judgments create authority on a general basis), and critique the balancing act that must be performed in judgments between the ability of an individual to manifest their religious beliefs, and the protections which anti-discrimination laws provide to the general population. The courts in the UK must interpret the **Equality Act 2010** to conform with the spirit of, and to give effect to, the **ECHR**.

Alternative forms of dispute resolution

The courts and tribunals are important features of the English legal system for obvious reasons. However, remember that they are not the only—nor indeed necessarily should they be considered the primary—forum for resolving disputes. In business relationships and intra-organizational disputes, the adversarial court system may prove disastrous and a more conciliatory approach to dispute resolution may save relationships—particularly important in the current economic climate. Further, parties who ignore ADR may find court costs applied which can be particularly expensive. Consider *Saigol v Thorney Ltd* [2014] as a cautionary tale. Here a minor dispute involving claim and counter-claim led to awards to the parties (respectively) of £745 and £375. As mediation did not resolve their dispute, the parties proceeded to court where they incurred legal costs of £67,000 and £77,000—a total of £144,000. As neither party made seemingly genuine and reasonable attempts to settle the claim, they were each liable for their own legal costs. Thus, alternative forms of dispute resolution should be explored and carefully considered.

Forms of ADR

There are many approaches to ADR including internal dispute resolution techniques, negotiations, the ombudsman scheme, and so on. This is a very broad topic but commonly used mechanisms include arbitration, conciliation, and mediation.

Arbitration

This is a voluntary system of ADR and involves the parties relying on the services of an arbitrator who is an independent, fair, and impartial third party, and who is often legally trained or is an expert in the subject matter of the dispute. The hearings under arbitration have the benefit of being private and hence in business, a firm's actions, or contractual dealings, financial records, and so on are not subject to public scrutiny.

Conciliation

This process is similar to mediation, however the conciliator adopts a more proactive role. Their role is to offer solutions and identify strategies for the successful resolution of the dispute. An example of its use can be seen through the intervention of the Advisory, Conciliation and Arbitration Service in dismissals in employment. See Chapter 8.

Mediation

Mediation may be 'evaluative' (where an assessment is made of the 'legal' issues of the subject forming the dispute) or it can involve a 'facilitative approach' (where the emphasis is on assisting the parties to resolve their differences in a mutually acceptable way). The parties appoint the mediator and where the process is successful in establishing a resolution, this may form the basis of a legally binding agreement, unless there is a provision between the parties that such agreements are not to be binding.

Several of the advantages noted in Table 1.3 are context-specific, and it should not be underestimated that some claimants will want 'their day in court' and do not want to mediate a resolution.

Key cases

****

Table 1.3 Features of ADR

Advantages of ADR	Disadvantages of ADR
A cooperative approach	Absence of legal protection
Speed of resolution	Possible duplication of fees
Lower costs	Absence of legal expertise
Expertise of arbitrators	Lack of use
Informality	Imbalance and abuse of power relations
Increased compliance with orders	
Privacy of proceedings	

✓ **Looking for extra marks?**

In an attempt to resolve trader–consumer disputes without court action, a voluntary system was introduced from October 2015. The **Alternative Dispute Resolution for Consumer Disputes (Competent Authorities and Information) Regulations 2015** requires traders, having failed to resolve a dispute through internal dispute resolution measures, to inform the consumer of a relevant ADR body (known as a 'competent authority'—such as the Financial Conduct Authority, Legal Services Board, and Gas and Electricity Markets Authority) with whom a dispute can be lodged. The requirements for online dispute resolution for consumer disputes have been addressed through the **Alternative Dispute Resolution for Consumer Disputes (Amendment) (No 2) Regulations 2015**. In any assessment of the Regulations remember that, whilst the trader is not compelled to use the body, by putting the onus on the trader to inform the consumer, they may at least be knowledgeable about the existence of ADR and the benefits it can bring in relation to maintaining good commercial relationships—and hence possibly be more likely to use ADR.

(✱) **Key cases**

Case	Facts	Principle
Commission v UK (Case 61/81) [1982] ICR 578	The UK had to amend the Equal Pay Act 1970 to ensure that the Equal Pay Directive was correctly transposed. This required the inclusion of a 'third head' of complaint—'work of equal value'.	Domestic law, when interpreted in light of EU law, was found to be incompatible. Therefore legislative action was taken to ensure individuals had access to the protection that EU law required.

Case	Facts	Principle
Factortame [1991] 1 AC 603	A domestic law was enacted that contravened an EU treaty Article.	There was no authority for the judiciary to disapply an Act of Parliament. However, when faced with applying a domestic law that clearly breached EU law, the CJEU stated that the courts had to prevent its application. This was a fundamental change in the constitution.
Re Sigsworth [1935] Ch 89	A beneficiary of a dead woman's estate was also the man who had killed her.	A strict, literal interpretation of the relevant legislation provided no restriction on the man's ability to benefit from his action. However, as a matter of public policy, the golden rule of interpretation was used to avoid the result a literal interpretation would have provided.
Smith v Hughes [1960] 1 WLR 830	To circumvent legislation prohibiting prostitution in a street or public place, a prostitute solicited from within her house.	As the legislation had been enacted to stop the mischief of prostitution, the court interpreted this to include soliciting in a street *and* in a person's own home.

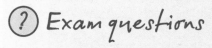 ? Exam questions

Problem question

Advanced Electronics Ltd (AEL) is a private limited company which has experienced the following situation and requires appropriate advice to ensure an effective resolution. AEL has a significant corporate customer, BigByte Ltd, which regularly places very large orders with it. However, a problem has started to develop. While AEL provides BigByte with a standard trade credit period of 'full payment within 30 days', BigByte has got into the habit of paying late (sometimes as late as 90 days). AEL's concern is that if other trade customers get to know that they are being relaxed about making BigByte pay on time then they may ask for similar extended credit periods. AEL has considered increasing the price of goods sold to BigByte so as to 'charge' the company for the additional credit but fears that any increase in price will merely result in this valued customer going elsewhere.

Advise AEL about alternative forms of dispute resolution (ADR) that could be used to resolve this situation. Specifically identify the advantages ADR may provide compared with traditional court action in relation to business relationships.

An outline answer is included at the end of the book.

Exam questions

✳✳✳✳✳✳✳✳✳✳

Essay question

The courts do not provide swift justice. They are very slow, allow for parties to delay and waste time, and redress through the courts can involve the use of qualified lawyers who charge significant sums of money. This system benefits the rich and those who have the resources to wait for an outcome/ award to be made (such as employers).

The tribunal system sought to redress the balance of power and provide a speedy, cost-effective, and informal mechanism to resolve workplace disputes. They removed the advantages held by employers in disputes with (more vulnerable) employees.

Critically assess the statement given and comment on whether employment tribunals have provided the advantages identified, compared with the traditional court system. Justify your answer with reference to any changes in the law and tribunal procedure you feel are relevant.

 Online Resources

To see an outline answer to this question log on to www.oup.com/lawrevision/

#2

Contract I: essential features of a contract

Key facts

- Offer and acceptance are the first stages in establishing an agreement that may form a legally binding contract. The terms that will bind the parties are included here.

- Offers may appear similar to an invitation to treat (which is an invitation to negotiate) but they must be distinguished so as to determine the offeror and to whom an offer is made.

- Generally, items on display on the shelves in a shop, advertisements in newspapers, items displaying a price tag in shop windows, and information in auction catalogues have been held to be invitations to treat.

- An offer may be accepted at any point until it is terminated.

- Acceptance can only be made by the offeree or their agent.

- Consideration is the bargain element of a contract and may be referred to as the 'price of a promise'.

- Consideration must be legally sufficient but need not be adequate.

- The parties must intend for an agreement to establish legal relations to create an enforceable contract. Presumptions exist in relation to social/domestic agreements and business/commercial agreements.

- The courts will look to the actions of the parties to identify terms of a contract. When preparing a written contract, careful drafting is necessary as the courts will not rewrite a poorly drafted agreement.

Essential features of a contract

The following features must be present in a contract to make it legally enforceable (see Fig 2.1).

Unilateral and bilateral contracts

Bilateral contracts are those where one of the parties offers to do something in return for an action by the other party—they exchange promises. For example, one person agrees to wash the other's car in return for having their lawn mowed. Acceptance of the offer must be communicated for an agreement to be established.

A unilateral contract is one where the first party promises to perform some action in return for a specific act, although the second party is not promising to take any action. Acceptance may take effect through conduct and need not be communicated. For example, in *Carlill v Carbolic Smoke Ball Co* [1893] the Carbolic Smoke Ball Co (the first party) advertised its product and stated that it would pay customers £100 if they contracted influenza after using the smoke ball as directed. Carlill (the second party) was under no obligation to enter the contract, nor was she required to communicate her acceptance of the offer. The contract was only formed when Carlill took the action (ie her conduct) to accept.

Figure 2.1 Essential features of a valid contract

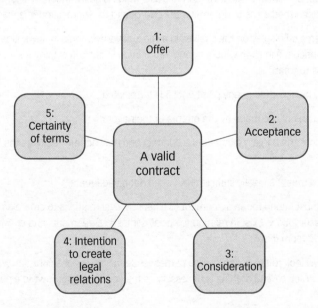

Offer

An offer is a set of terms under which the **offeror** (the party making the offer) is willing to be bound. An offer is made to the **offeree** (the recipient of the offer) who must accept in the method expressed (if stipulated) by the offeror.

Revision tip

Typical questions can include differentiating between an offer and an invitation to treat. This is a vital distinction and requires reference to key cases. Problem questions are often used and may follow a similar form to the facts in case law—adverts in shop windows or newspapers/items on the shelves in retail outlets, and so on.

Invitation to treat

An invitation to treat is a willingness to accept offers or enter into negotiations. In this context, the word 'treat' means to negotiate, and hence it can be viewed as an invitation to negotiate for a good or service (see Fig 2.2). The justification for invitation to treat is pragmatic as, without it, retailers would be making standing offers to the whole world which, if they were unable to fulfil, would result in a breach. Examples can be seen where traders sell goods through advertisements, auctions, and negotiations.

Pharmaceutical Society of Great Britain v Boots Cash Chemists **[1953] 2 WLR 427**

Boots Chemists operated a 'self-service' system involving the customer tendering their selection to a cashier; it amounted to an offer by the customer to buy rather than an offer by Boots to sell. As such, items displayed on shelves are generally held to be an invitation to treat and *not* an offer to sell.

Exceptions do exist, and where greater details are present in adverts with regards to price, quantity, availability, etc, then an advert can amount to an offer rather than an invitation to treat (see *Leftkowitz v Great Minneapolis Surplus Stores* [1957]—although this is a judgment from the United States and is of persuasive authority only).

✓ Looking for extra marks?

Include in an answer on offer/invitation to treat the *Leftkowitz* case and explain the difference between displaying goods (invitation to treat) and identifying specific details of quantity and availability of goods (that may indicate an offer).

Items in shop windows displayed with a price tag (*Fisher v Bell* [1960]) are also held as invitations to treat. Such an approach is necessary to prevent a shop from displaying goods with an incorrect price tag attached and then being compelled to proceed with the contract on the basis of an innocent mistake.

Invitation to treat
✳✳✳✳✳✳✳✳✳✳✳

Figure 2.2 An example of an invitation to treat

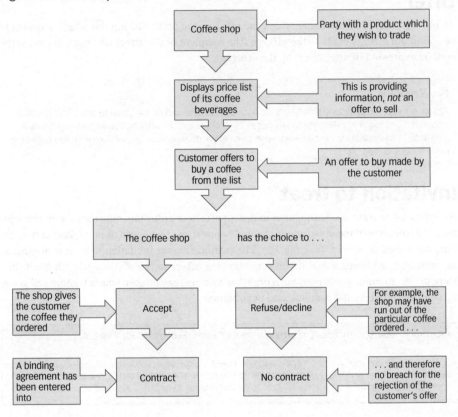

Advertisements are a potentially problematic area, because the words used can lead buyers to assume an offer has been made. The courts will often interpret advertisements in newspapers, magazines, and journals as an invitation to treat. With advertisements generally, whether these are through television, radio, or the internet, the same rules apply (*Partridge v Crittenden* [1968]).

Negotiations occur between parties in the contract process. Questions of item, price, quantity, and the terms surrounding any possible contract may come under consideration by the parties. This can lead to disagreements as to when an offer may have been made which is capable of acceptance. The courts have had to look to the parties' statements and other evidence to ascertain their true intentions (*Harvey v Facey* [1893]).

Mere negotiations between parties are insufficient to create a contract and the courts will not imply an offer in these situations. Similarly, a request for information will not amount to an offer capable of acceptance, or be considered a counter-offer that would destroy the offer.

Gibson v Manchester CC [1979] 1 WLR 294

Gibson was a tenant and occupier of a council house. The Council wrote to Gibson informing him that it might be willing to sell the property and Gibson responded that he wished to go ahead with the purchase. When political control of the Council changed, the policy of 'right to buy' was revoked. Gibson claimed a breach of contract as the Council refused to conclude the sale but the House of Lords held that the Council never made an offer to sell and hence Gibson's actions could not amount to valid acceptance. All that had occurred in this case were the first steps towards negotiations for a sale which never reached fruition.

Revision tip

When using *Gibson v Manchester CC* as precedent for the distinction between an offer and a request for information it is always worthwhile to compare the decision with *Storer v Manchester CC* [1974]. *Storer* demonstrates where the negotiations have proceeded to a formal offer being made.

Termination of an offer

An offer may be terminated as a result of the actions of the parties or by expiry due to the passage of time. It is advisable for the offeror to include terms as to when the offer will expire. This prevents confusion and the necessity of interpretation by the courts.

The following are examples of how an offer can be terminated:

- The offeror's death: non-acceptance of an offer before the offeror's death will result in the termination of the offer. If the offer has been accepted before the offeror dies, where practicable the contract must still be performed (by the dead person's estate or executors—*Bradbury v Morgan* [1862]). This will not apply to contracts involving personal service (here the contract will be frustrated).

- Expiry of a fixed time limit: if the time limit for acceptance expires, then the offer dies and cannot later be accepted.

- Acceptance within a reasonable time: a contract may include a time limit after which the offer will expire. Where none exists, the offer will automatically expire within a reasonable time (which is dependent on the facts of the case). See *Ramsgate Victoria Hotel v Montefiore* (1865–66).

- Rejection: where the offeree rejects the offer it is destroyed (this can be explicit in words or through their conduct).

- A counter-offer: negotiations involve offers and counter-offers, but a counter-offer acts to 'kill the original offer' (*Hyde v Wrench* [1840]).

Acceptance

****

> ### *Hyde v Wrench* [1840] 3 Beav 334
>
> An offer of the sale of property was answered with a counter-offer of a lower amount. This counter-offer destroyed the first offer so the original offer could not later be accepted.

- Revocation: the offeror may revoke the offer at any time before it is accepted—even where they have promised to keep the offer open for a specific period of time (insofar as it is communicated by the offeror/reliable third party—*Dickinson v Dodds* (1875–76)). If such an element appears in an examination question, remember to identify the exception to this general rule where the offeree has provided **consideration** for the offer remaining open.

In situations of 'unilateral' contracts the option to revoke the offer may be more difficult. For example, in *Carlill* [1893], it would be quite unrealistic to communicate the revocation to every person who may have seen the advertisement in a newspaper, but taking reasonable steps (such as another advertisement in the same newspaper revoking the offer) may be acceptable.

Acceptance

The acceptance of the offeror's terms must be unconditional. In many cases this may constitute a 'yes' or 'no' reply to an offer made. There are situations where such a simple exercise may not be possible and it requires the courts to give direction as to how acceptance may be established. An offer may be accepted by conduct; silence, however, will not constitute acceptance in bilateral contracts.

> ### *Novus Aviation Limited v Alubaf Arab International Bank BSC(c)* [2016] EWHC 1575 (Comm)
>
> A commitment letter had been exchanged and signed by one of the parties. The other had not signed it but, before withdrawing from the deal, the parties had incorporated new companies, opened bank accounts, and appointed directors to facilitate the contract. On the withdrawal, a claim of repudiatory breach was made. The Commercial Court held a binding contract had been made on the basis of the parties' conduct. There was no requirement for the commitment letter to be signed—a situation which could have been avoided through an express requirement.

Communication of acceptance

For a valid contract to exist the terms of the offer must be accepted by the offeree. This means:

- outward evidence of the offeree's intention to accept an offer has to be demonstrated (in unilateral and bilateral contracts) and communicated (in bilateral contracts) in order for effective acceptance;

- silence is not effective acceptance (*Felthouse v Bindley* [1862]);

- the offeree may deviate in the method of acceptance stipulated in the offer if the alternative method is as fast or quicker than that in the offer (*Yates Building Co Ltd v R J Pulleyn & Sons Ltd* [1975]);

- acceptance may be evidenced through conduct (such as in *Carlill* [1893]). In *Alexander Brogden v Metropolitan Railway Co* [1877] a contractual document had been drafted by the **principals** of the companies and was used in negotiations between the parties. Whilst it had not been signed, it was sufficient that the intentions from the parties' actions enabled an agreement to be deduced.

Postal rule of acceptance

The general rule established with the post is that acceptance is effective on posting, not on the receipt of the acceptance. This applies insofar as the correct address and postage were used in the sent letter (*Adams v Lindsell* [1818]).

The postal rule is not effective, however, in situations where the express terms of the contract state that the acceptance must be received and in writing. In *Holwell Securities v Hughes* [1974] Lawton LJ stated that the postal rule would not be used where to do so would 'produce manifest inconvenience and absurdity'.

Revision tip

Always be aware that the postal rule is only applicable where the post is a valid means of acceptance. If the parties have expressly provided that it will not be considered as valid acceptance, or where the parties require the acceptance to be received in writing, then the standard rule of communication remains.

Instantaneous communication

Compared with the postal rule, in cases involving instantaneous forms of communication, the courts have traditionally reverted to the common rule of acceptance being effective when communicated and received (*Entores v Miles Far East Corporation* [1955] and *Brinkibon v Stahag Stahl und Stahlwarenhandels GmbH* [1982]).

Consideration

Consideration is a necessary component of all contracts (unless the contract is made by deed). Consideration in contract law is merely something of value that is provided and which acts as the inducement to enter into the agreement. The definition most definitively used is from the seminal case *Currie v Misa* (1874–75) but it is sufficient at this stage to recognize consideration as the bargain element of a contract—'the price of a promise' or 'the badge of enforceability'.

Consideration

Consideration must be given in return for the promise made, and it must move from the **promisee** (the party who wishes to enforce the contract must provide (or have provided) consideration). The promisee may exchange promises with the **promisor**, or they may provide some act or forbearance, to establish good consideration (see Fig 2.3).

***

Rock Advertising Ltd v MWB Business Exchange Centres Ltd [2018] UKSC 24

The case involved Rock, which had run into difficulties paying its monthly licence fees on office space owned by MWB. An oral agreement was reached between MWB's credit controller and a director of Rock for a rescheduling of the payments (at a lower rate for a period of months). The licence agreement included a clause that 'all variations to this licence must be agreed, set out in writing and signed on behalf of both parties before they take effect'. Despite the clause, the Court of Appeal held the oral agreement was enforceable. Under the principle of freedom of contract the parties may agree whatever terms they choose (including the variation of such terms). The agreement was also supported by fresh consideration which made it binding—the defendant would not have empty premises or have to seek legal action to recover the rent. However, the Supreme Court reversed the Court of Appeal's judgment. Such 'no oral modification' clauses prevent parties from being exploited and, on the Court of Appeal's point regarding the concept of freedom of contract, it also allowed the parties to agree to bind their future conduct. The Supreme Court has thus returned the certainty of such clauses but did question whether the law on consideration needed re-examination.

***

The two types of consideration are executed and executory.

Executed

Executed consideration is often seen in unilateral contracts and involves one party making a promise in return for an act by the other party. The offeror has no obligation to take action on the contract until the other party has fulfilled their part (eg A offers B £100 to build a wall, payment to be made on completion). B completes the building work and is entitled to the payment from A. If B did not want the work, or did not complete it, A would not have paid the £100.

Executory

Executory consideration is performed after an offer is made and is an act to be performed in the future (hence executory)—it is an exchange of promises to perform an act. This form of consideration is frequently seen in bilateral contracts and may lead to a valid contract being established (eg X orders a computer with the promise to pay for it on delivery, and Y promises to deliver the computer and receive the payment). The fact that consideration has not yet occurred but will take place in the future does not prevent it being 'good' consideration and in the event of, for example, non-delivery, this may lead to a breach of contract—assuming the remainder of the essential features are present.

Figure 2.3 Good consideration

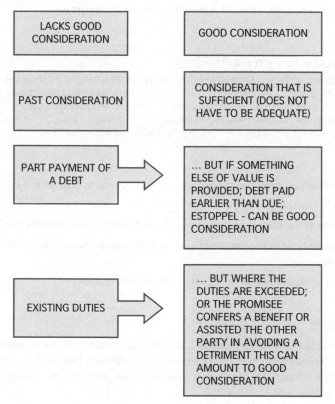

Other factors in consideration

Consideration must be sufficient (not adequate)

Consideration must have some legal, material value but it does not need to be adequate in relation to a 'fair' price for the contract. Per Blackburn J in *Bolton v Madden* [1873] 'the adequacy of the consideration is for the parties to consider at the time of making the agreement, not for the Court'.

Consideration must not be past

Where a promise is made after the completion of an act, that act itself is not sufficient to provide consideration to enforce the promise. The promisor is not obtaining a benefit for their promise—the benefit has already been received (*Re McArdle, Decd* [1951]) and will be held a *nudum pactum* (a promise made with no consideration to support it).

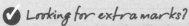

Looking for extra marks?

Compare this general rule with *Lampleigh v Brathwaite* [1615], where the defendant, who had killed another person, requested the claimant to obtain a pardon from the King. Lampleigh was successful and, as a result, Brathwaite made a promise to pay £100 for the service, but this payment was never made. It was held that Lampleigh was able to recover the £100 because the court felt that both parties must have contemplated that payment for the service would be made.

The following are necessary to claim an enforceable contract exists with past consideration:

- the act that is the subject of the contract must have been requested by the promisor;
- it must have been in the contemplation of both parties that payment would have been made; and
- all the other elements of a valid contract must have existed.

Existing duties

Consideration must be 'real and material' and, as such, if the promisor is merely receiving what they are already entitled to, then there is no consideration furnished (*Collins v Godefroy* [1831]). The Privy Council held in *Pao On v Lau Yiu Long* [1980] that an existing duty owed to a third party can be good consideration.

The 'existing duties' rule seeks to ensure that improper pressure cannot be applied to renegotiate a contract on better terms for the promisee. In *Stilk v Myrick* [1809], the captain of a vessel on a voyage promised the existing crew an equal share of the wages of two seamen who had deserted (and who could not be replaced). The wages were not provided, and in the action to recover the wages, the court held that there was no consideration provided in support of the promise. The seamen were under an existing duty to 'exert themselves to the utmost to bring the ship in safely to her destined port'.

Stilk v Myrick has to be compared with *Hartley v Ponsonby* [1857] where the sailors in this case were promised additional money if they completed their voyage after half of the ship's crew had abandoned the vessel. The court held that they were entitled to the extra pay as they exceeded their existing duties due to the significant risk of continuing the voyage with insufficient crew.

Note: performance of an existing duty may be held as good consideration where the promisee has actually conferred on the promisor a benefit or has assisted them in avoiding a detriment, and no unfair pressure or **duress** was used in the renegotiation.

Williams v Roffey Bros & Nicholls (Contractors) Ltd [1991] 1 QB 1

Roffey Bros, building contractors, entered into a contract with a housing association to refurbish a block of flats. Roffey subcontracted various carpentry jobs to Williams who could not complete the work as his agreed price was too low to enable him to operate at a profit. Williams informed Roffey that he would be unable to complete the work and Roffey agreed to pay to Williams a further sum in excess of the original for the work to be completed at the agreed date (this would assist Roffey, among other reasons, to avoid delay penalties). On completion, Roffey refused to pay the additional money on the basis that Williams had only performed an existing duty.

The Court of Appeal held that the promise to pay the additional sum was binding. Despite Roffey's argument to the contrary, consideration was provided as Roffey did receive a benefit, or at the very least would avoid a detriment, through the completion of the work and the avoidance of the penalty fee and/or the difficulty in hiring a new subcontractor.

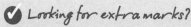 **Looking for extra marks?**

Identify the importance of the decision in *Williams v Roffey* in which it appeared the requirement for a variation of the contract had to be supported by fresh consideration. However, note its limitation to obligations for debt and in particular compare with the cases *Re Selectmove* [1995] and *Foakes v Beer* (1884).

Part payment as consideration

As a general rule, part payment of a debt will not prevent the party owed money from later claiming the balance (*Pinnel's Case* (1602)).

Exceptions to the rule regarding part payment:

- if the party has paid a lower amount, but has done so at an earlier date, then this may amount to good consideration;
- if there have been goods or another benefit provided along with the lower payment then this may also provide good consideration; and
- the major exception to this rule, alongside the others noted, is the doctrine of **promissory estoppel**.

Doctrine of promissory estoppel

The rule of part payment not being good consideration was established through the common law, but courts also created an equitable defence which stops a party that has made a (gratuitous) promise from reneging. Essentially, it seeks to suspend rights rather than to extinguish them (although this is a moot point in many instances—see *Tool Metal Manufacturing Co v Tungsten Ltd* [1955]).

Consideration

✳✳✳✳✳✳✳✳✳✳✳✳

Central London Property Trust v High Trees House Ltd [1956] 1 All ER 256
High Trees House leased a block of flats from Central London Property Trust in 1937. With the outbreak of war, and the consequent bombings in London, occupancy of the property was reduced. In order to reduce the adverse effects, including it being unoccupied, High Trees entered into a new agreement under which the rent would be reduced by half. In 1945, the flats were fully occupied and Central London Property claimed for the full rent to be paid. The High Court held that when the flats became fully let, the full rent could be claimed. However, Denning J stated (**obiter dicta**) that any attempt to claim the balance of rent from 1940 to 1945 would not be allowed under the doctrine of promissory estoppel as High Trees relied on the promise made not to claim the full rent.

This is an unusual case and its rule was made *obiter*, so this limits its reliance as a precedent; however, here a promise was enforceable even though unsupported by consideration. This was because of the existing relationship between the parties: the parties had intended to (and in fact did) act upon the agreement, and the promisor intended to create legal relations.

Revision tip

Promissory estoppel is a complicated area of law and cases exist that challenge the application of the doctrine. In a question involving promissory estoppel, knowledge and critique of these cases will ensure the highest marks. Further, highlight the uncertainty of whether its use removes the obligations completely or whether they may be reintroduced following reasonable notice. Consider cases such as *Hughes v Metropolitan Railway Co* (1877) and *Jorden v Money* (1854) when explaining the judgment of Denning J in the *High Trees* case.

Note the limitation of the doctrine:

- it may only be used as a shield not a sword (ie as a defence to an action);
- as an equitable remedy, it is not available to a party who has acted inequitably.

Promissory estoppel would potentially allow for the enforcement of an agreement to accept a portion of a debt in full settlement and this possibility has been acknowledged in *Collier v P & MJ Wright (Holdings) Ltd* [2007].

Consideration is often linked with the concept of privity of contract, where the contract involves, or is for the benefit of, a third party. This is because that party (even though the contract concerns them) has not provided any consideration and hence (traditionally) has no rights or obligations under the agreement.

Privity of contract

The doctrine establishes that only parties to a contract may sue or be sued on it, and consequently provides rights and imposes obligations on those parties alone. This is important as many situations involve contracts where a right or benefit is to be provided for a third party (although consumer contracts may allow for a third party to enforce a contract made specifically for their benefit).

The two elements necessary to enforce a contract are:

- the claimant must be a party to it (*Dunlop Tyre Co v Selfridge* [1915]) and
- there must be consideration provided by the promisee (*Tweddle v Atkinson* [1861]).

Privity of contract could, in certain circumstances, produce unfairness and inconvenience to the parties. As a consequence, the common law has created many exceptions such as agency; collateral contracts; trusts; insurance contracts; restrictive covenants; and contracts for interested groups. Statutory action also provided for third party action on a contract.

Intention to create legal relations

'Legal relations' means that the parties view the agreement as a legally enforceable contract and a breach of the contract could result in a remedy being sought. The existence of 'legal relations' can be examined in terms of the sphere in which they might originate: social/domestic or business/commercial (see Fig 2.4).

Social/domestic

Here, the presumption is that the parties do not **intend to create legal relations**. In *Balfour v Balfour* [1919] an agreement between a husband and wife regarding payment for the wife's

Figure 2.4 Presumptions regarding intention to create legal relations

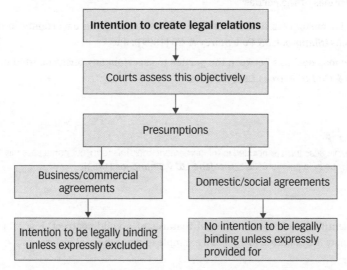

maintenance was considered not to be legally binding. However, the presumption involving a married couple is not made when they are separated (*Merritt v Merritt* [1970]).

This presumption against the creation of legal relations applies to arrangements involving friends and social acquaintances where a prior history exists between the parties (*Hadley and Others v Kemp and Another* [1999]).

Where such parties make an outward sign that they intend the agreement to be legally binding, this will be effective and reverse the presumption (*Simpkins v Pays* [1955]).

Business/commercial

Between commercial parties, intention to create legal relations is presumed unless the parties establish an agreement to the contrary (*Rose and Frank Company v J R Crompton* [1925]).

Revision Tip

Remember the presumptions, but also look out for expressed intentions that either a business/commercial agreement is to be 'in honour' only and hence not legally binding, or conversely, that a social/domestic agreement intends to be legally binding.

Certainty of terms

The terms of the contract must be certain if they are to be considered sufficiently precise to be enforced by a court. The courts will not rewrite a contract which has been incorrectly or negligently drafted. However, the courts use the following tactics to identify the terms and the true intentions of the parties:

- particular customs in a trade that may assist in removing uncertainty in the parties' intentions (*Shamrock SS Co v Storey & Co* [1899]); and
- the previous dealings between the parties to ascertain any terms omitted in a contract (*Hillas & Co Ltd v Arcos Ltd* [1932]).

Revision Tip

Where a meaningless term is included in the agreement, then this term, but not necessarily the entire contract, may be held unenforceable (*Nicolene Ltd v Simmonds* [1953]).

Having identified each of the essential features of a valid contract, Fig 2.5 provides an example of how they operate in a typical example of a purchase at a store.

Figure 2.5 Putting the stages together

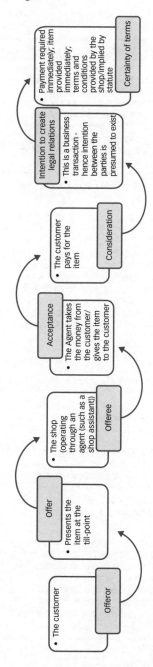

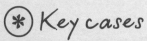

Case	Facts	Principle
Carlill v Carbolic Smoke Ball Co [1893] 1 QB 256	The defendant advertised a £100 reward to anyone who used its smoke ball and contracted influenza. The Court of Appeal held this to amount to a unilateral offer which was accepted when an individual used the product as directed. When Carlill brought an action for the reward, the defendant claimed, *inter alia*, that the offer was a 'mere puff'.	The Court of Appeal held a valid contract was in existence and the £100 was payable. The advertisement amounted to a unilateral offer, and the contract was formed through acceptance by the claimant's conduct (no communication was required). The monies deposited in a bank for the settlement of potential claims demonstrated the sincerity of the defendants which went beyond mere advertising puff.
Hyde v Wrench [1840] 3 Beav 334	Wrench offered to sell land for £1,000 to Hyde. Hyde replied with 'acceptance' of the offer of sale at a price of £950. This was rejected. Later, Hyde attempted to accept the original offer and pay £1,000 for the land, but this was rejected.	Upon an action for breach of contract it was held that if Hyde had unconditionally accepted Wrench's offer to sell at £1,000 an enforceable contract would have been established. The £950 was not valid acceptance (which has to be an unequivocal acceptance of the offeror's terms) and instead this action had (implicitly) rejected (and destroyed) the first offer, which made it impossible to accept at a later date.
Pharmaceutical Society of Great Britain v Boots Cash Chemists [1953] 2 WLR 427	An action was brought against Boots on the basis that a contract of sale was concluded when a customer placed items in their shopping basket—and these sales were contrary to statute.	Items displayed on shelves are an invitation to treat. The customer tenders these to the cashier offering to purchase, and the seller (trader) may choose to accept or decline this offer.
Rose and Frank Company v J R Crompton [1925] AC 445	Two companies began trading with a third company. The three companies entered into an agreement regarding sales and purchases incorporating a clause that the agreement was 'in honour' only and not legally enforceable.	The House of Lords held that the arrangement had not created a binding contract because of the 'in honour' clause which had removed this essential feature.

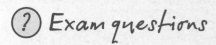 Exam questions

Problem question

Gordon works as a salesman in the Orange Computers Inc store. His contract of employment provides for an annual salary of £25,000 and commission payments (at 7 per cent) on any computers and peripherals he sells. In the previous three years the commission payments have amounted to an average of £19,000.

The world economic downturn adversely affected the store. The manager, Fred, informed Gordon that the business was in severe financial trouble and that he must reduce the firm's outgoings. In response, Fred asked Gordon if he would forgo his salary for 2017, 2018, and 2019, and accept payments of commission only. Fred explained to Gordon that this was required of him (and all other staff) or the business would probably not survive and it would have to be wound up owing substantial debts to creditors. As such, Gordon accepted the variation of the contract.

In 2017 the economy began to grow, and in small part due to governmental incentives for investment in information technology, the store managed to trade its way through the difficult times and is making a healthy profit. As such, Gordon feels that he should be able to receive his wages for 2019 and not simply have to rely on his commission as agreed in 2017. He also wishes to know if he can successfully claim for his wages from 2017 and 2018 as Orange Computers Inc has sufficient profits to repay this money.

Advise Gordon whether he can obtain his wages for 2019, and also whether he would have any claim for the wages he agreed not to accept in the years 2017 and 2018. (Restrict your answer to the contractual issues rather than any employment obligations that may be present.)

An outline answer is included at the end of the book.

Essay question

Compare and contrast the approach taken by the courts when determining the acceptance of an offer through the post and using instantaneous forms of communication. Why were opposing rules established and what impact does this have for the parties?

 Online Resources

To see an outline answer to this question log on to www.oup.com/lawrevision/

#3

Contract II: mistake, misrepresentation, duress, and undue influence

Key facts

- The law imposes restrictions on certain persons (such as minors) when forming a contract.

- A fundamental mistake can make a contract void.

- There is no definite definition of a term, but the courts have identified various tests to differentiate a term from a representation.

- A contract formed on the basis of misrepresentation will make the contract voidable, but the innocent party must act promptly if they wish to repudiate.

- Duress and undue influence affect the validity of a contract.

Introduction

Once a contract has been formed, questions may be raised regarding how the agreement was concluded that could affect its validity. For example, one party may have induced the other to enter the contract by misrepresenting an important aspect of the contract; there may have been a mistake as to the party contracting; or one party may have exerted undue influence in the conclusion of an agreement. It is necessary to identify if any of these important elements are present in the agreement which could affect the contract or its validity. If present, there are a number of remedies available to the innocent party.

Revision tip

Examination questions can include any of the aspects covered in this chapter, but they will most likely involve misrepresentation and/or mistake. As a business law subject, the examination may involve an aspect of misrepresentation and mistake where a **rogue** purchases goods on credit from a trader. Clearly, such questions lend themselves to a problem scenario, and it is important to:

* recognize which law is relevant;
* appreciate the effects on the agreement (is the 'contract' void, voidable, or unenforceable?); and
* identify the remedies available.

Capacity to contract

For parties to establish a legally enforceable agreement, they must possess the capacity to contract.

Minors

Minors (persons under 18 years of age) have the capacity to establish most contracts. However, situations exist where the minor requires protection and in those situations the contract established may be voidable, hence allowing the minor the ability to avoid the contract.

Voidable contracts

* Contracts involving the sale of shares (*Steinberg v Scala (Leeds) Ltd* [1923]);
* leasing property; and
* contracts of partnership.

Where the minor will be bound by the contract

* Where the contract is not unduly harsh or detrimental to the minor, it will be binding; and
* If the contract is for the benefit of the minor, and does not place unfair responsibility on them, it will be enforceable (*Clements v London and North Western Railway Co* [1894]).

Mental incapacity

Persons who have been identified with a mental incapacity, and are defined under the **Mental Capacity Act 2005** as a 'patient', are protected from entering contracts and any agreements purporting to be a contract will be void.

> *Revision tip*
>
> In questions involving patients' agreements, remember that the 'contract' will be held void even if the other party is unaware of the patient's incapacity.

Where the person is not considered to be a patient under the relevant legislation, to avoid the contract the mentally ill person must demonstrate that at the time of concluding the contract they did not understand the nature of the agreement, and the other party must or should have known of the mental incapacity present.

Intoxication

A person who is under the influence of alcohol or drugs when a contract is concluded is generally bound by the contract. It is presumed by the courts that they are aware of their actions. This presumption is reversed, and the contract is voidable, if the party is so intoxicated that they do not know the consequences of the agreement they are concluding, and the other party is aware.

Mistake

A contract may be held void due to a fundamental mistake, as the parties did not have a true agreement. However, it is distinct from where the parties may have erroneously entered into a contract that is a bad bargain, or where one party later has 'second thoughts'. In such circumstances, the contract will not be void.

Remember, mistake is not concerned with the attributes of a particular item, such as buying a printer for a computer under the misapprehension that it had a scanner facility as well (unless this feature was misrepresented to the buyer).

In order for the mistake to enable the contract to be void, it must be both fundamental and 'operative' which prevents the *consensus ad idem* (meeting of minds) that is an essential feature of a valid contract.

Common mistake

Here the parties have made the same fundamental mistake when reaching agreement. Examples of mistake, and its effect can be seen in the following cases:

The subject matter of the agreement is no longer in existence when the contract is established

> **Couturier v Hastie [1856] 5 HL Cases 673**
>
> The contract concerned the sale of goods (in this case it was for corn), but whilst the negotiations were proceeding, the carrier of the goods disposed of it. It was held that there could be no contract as the goods subject to the negotiation were not available when the contract was concluded.

Mistakes as to the existence of the subject matter make the contract void.

However, being careless in a negotiation is not the same as an operative mistake and such a party may be liable for breach of contract.

Mistake as to quality (of the subject matter)

> **Bell v Lever Bros Ltd [1932] AC 161 (HL)**
>
> An employee of the company was dismissed for redundancy with a compensatory payment being provided. However, prior to the payment and at the time unknown to the employer, the employee had breached the terms of the contract which would have allowed for his dismissal without compensation. The company attempted to recover the money paid but it was held that such a mistake was not void as to quality (it was not sufficiently different from that which the parties had in their contemplation) as it was not a fundamental mistake. Further, there was no misrepresentation that would have allowed a claim to recover the payment.

The Court of Appeal decided on the issue of equitable mistake in the following case:

> **Great Peace Shipping Ltd v Tsavliris Salvage International Ltd [2002] EWCA Civ 1407**
>
> The ship *Cape Providence* had sustained serious damage at sea. Tsavliris offered its salvage services and a contract was established. Tsavliris contacted a London broker to find a ship to assist and entered into the hire of the *Great Peace* (as the closest vessel) for a minimum of five days. However, the *Great Peace* was actually 400 miles away. It was discovered that another vessel was in closer proximity so the brokers were informed to cancel the contract for the *Great Peace* and establish a new contract with this closer ship. When payment was requested on the original contract, Tsavliris refused to pay for the hire of the *Great Peace* on the basis that the contract was void for common mistake.

It was held that there is no basis on which a contract is to be rescinded due to mutual mistake where, at common law, the contract is valid and enforceable.

Mistakes as to quality cannot make the contract voidable in equity.

Note that a common mistake in relation to the ownership of property will not result in the contract being void.

Mutual mistake—nature of the contract or its subject matter

Such mistakes are not common, but the following case provides an example:

Mistake

****

> ### *Raffles v Wichelhaus* [1864] 2 Hurl & C 906
>
> The parties contracted for the sale of cotton, which was the cargo on the ship the *Peerless*, sailing from Bombay. In fact there were two ships called the *Peerless* sailing with cotton from Bombay, and the parties were referring to different vessels. Therefore there could be no contract as the parties were mistaken as to the subject matter.

The court could not identify to which vessel the contract referred, therefore the contract was held void.

Unilateral mistake

The more common form of mistake is where one party is mistaken as to the terms of the contract or the identity of the other party.

Mistake as to the terms of the contract

Situations exist where the contract may be held void because the written contract contained contradictory information compared to the agreement established orally, and this is evident to the other party who attempts to rely on it—see *Hartog v Colin & Shields* [1939].

> *Revision tip*
>
> *Hartog* provides an example of how retailers who place incorrect prices on their goods are not bound by a customer's acceptance (assuming it was an offer not an invitation to treat). Where prices are clearly a mistake (eg a computer is advertised at £4.99 when its price obviously should have been £499) and the other party should reasonably have known this, no contract will be established.

Where a party has signed a document without reading it, the courts will not readily provide a remedy just because they later discover the content of the contract and disagree with it.

However, the courts have allowed a defence to be raised of *non est factum* (it is not my deed) but it cannot be used where:

* the signor has been careless or negligent in signing a document (*United Dominions Trust Ltd v Western* [1976]); or

* they signed a document the terms of which were not fundamentally or radically different from those which the signor thought they were signing; and

* they were negligent (in this respect careless) in the signing (*Lloyds Bank Plc v Waterhouse* [1991]).

The requirement of a fundamental or radical difference to the nature of the contract is somewhat harsh but is in line with the narrow use of the plea (*Gallie v Lee (Saunders v Anglia Building Society)* [1970]).

Mistake as to identity

The mistake as to the identity of the parties occurs where one party believes they are negotiating with a particular person, when in reality they are dealing with someone else.

Mistake in this area is linked with misrepresentation. Cases may involve a rogue obtaining possession of the victim's property and by doing so they obtain a voidable title to it (voidable for fraudulent misrepresentation). This title may be removed insofar as the victim takes steps to avoid the contract before the rogue passes the goods on (which they generally will wish to do so as to realize any value in the goods obtained). If the goods are transferred to a buyer purchasing them in good faith (an innocent third party), then good title transfers to the buyer. Hence the reason why the claimant will seek to establish the contract as void for mistake—the 'contract' never existed and therefore the rogue cannot pass on good title.

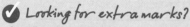

✔ Looking for extra marks?

When discussing the concept of good faith, remember there is no such general principle incorporated in contract law (it is present in agency relationships (including fiduciary obligations), some employment relations, and so on), but such a requirement was implied into a contract by the High Court in *Yam Seng Pte v International Trade Corporation* [2013]. This necessitated a broad interpretation of a good faith clause which the Court of Appeal, in *Mid Essex Hospital Services NHS Trust v Compass Group UK and Ireland Ltd (trading as Medirest)* [2013] rejected and considered that there was no need for the implication of good faith into the contract. When discussing issues of good faith it is wise to address both these cases and comment on the desirability of clear definition through contractual clauses to avoid the potential problems that implied terms have given rise to.

Revision tip

The courts will only allow a contract to be held void for mistake where:

- the rogue's identity was crucial to the conclusion of the contract;
- the parties had not met face-to-face; and
- the mistake must have concerned the other party's identity (who they were), not attributes (eg their creditworthiness).

Parties not meeting face-to-face

Cundy v Lindsay [1874–80] All ER Rep 1149

Blenkarn purported to be a sales representative of the firm Blenkiron & Sons. He previously hired property in the same street as the firm and had written to the claimants from this address seeking to obtain goods. Blenkarn entered into a contract through the post with the claimants for the purchase of a consignment of handkerchiefs, and sold these on without making payment. The court held that the claimants had intended to deal with Blenkiron, not Blenkarn, and as this was a fair mistake, the contract was void for mistake.

Mistake

✳✳✳✳✳✳✳✳✳✳✳✳

A key element in this judgment was that Lindsay was aware of the genuine and reputable firm (Blenkiron & Sons), and had provided the goods on credit due to the contract being, it believed, with this firm.

The parties' attributes

Cundy involved a mistake as to the party's identity, but the following case involved mistake as to creditworthiness.

> ### Kings Norton Metal Co Ltd v Edridge, Merrett & Co Ltd [1897] 14 TLR 98
>
> A company provided goods to a fraudster claiming to be a representative of a reputable firm and using correspondingly impressive company stationery. However, whereas in **Cundy** the firm existed and was reputable, here the firm did not exist and hence the mistake was to the attributes of the rogue rather than the party's identity. The company simply thought the rogue was creditworthy and therefore the rogue transferred ownership of the goods to the defendant. The claim for mistake failed.

The case demonstrated that mistake as to the attributes of the other party is insufficient to establish mistake. As the identity of the party was not crucial to the mistake, the contract was not void. The goods had been passed on to another buyer in good faith, and as there was no 'mistake' as to the rogue's identity, the claimants were not entitled to the return of the goods.

> ### ✅ Looking for extra marks?
>
> When discussing mistake as to identity, ensure you identify the key distinguishing features of *Cundy* and *Kings Norton*. Cundy mistakenly thought they were dealing with a previous customer, whilst Kings Norton were mistaken about the creditworthiness (attributes) of the rogue.

Parties meeting face-to-face

Where the parties have actually met in person, there is a strong presumption that it will prevent a claim for mistake as to identity (*Phillips v Brooks* [1919]). However this line of reasoning has to be considered in light of the House of Lords' decision in *Shogun Finance v Hudson* [2003].

> ### Shogun Finance Ltd v Hudson [2003] UKHL 62
>
> The case involved a rogue impersonating one Mr Patel for the purchase of a car. Mr Patel had no knowledge or involvement in the fraud, with the rogue producing documents of sufficient quality to convince a finance company of his assumed identity. The court held that the rogue had not obtained a good title to the car and it belonged to the finance company, not the innocent third party (Hudson) who had subsequently purchased it.

The key element in this judgment was the identity of the rogue. Here the finance company believed it was dealing with Mr Patel (through documentary evidence) and only intended to deal with Mr Patel. The company had performed adequate checks to verify this information and as such the contract between the rogue and the finance company was void. Therefore, title could not be passed on to Hudson.

Remedy of rectification

Rectification is an equitable remedy available in the case of mistake where a written agreement between the parties fails to reflect the actual agreement that was reached. The court has an option, if it believes that a contract did not reflect the true intentions of the parties at the time of the agreement, to have the relevant terms changed.

Distinguishing terms and representations

There are no strict rules as to what will constitute a **representation** and a term, but guidance is available from case law (see Table 3.1).

Table 3.1   Factors identifying terms and representations

Term	Statement	Representation
	Made by a party with actual or reasonably expected lesser knowledge of the contractual subject matter	(*Oscar Chess Ltd v Williams* [1957]) →
(*Bannerman v White* [1861]) ←	Reasonable reliance on statement made by the other party	
(*Schawel v Reade* [1913]) ←	Stronger/more empathic statements (unless statement cannot establish a term)	
←	Statement made close to the agreement (inducing the contract to be concluded)	

Misrepresentation

A written document will generally be considered to identify the terms of the contract. Those statements made during the course of negotiations that were not reduced to writing will generally be considered representations:

- a breach of a term will enable a claim for breach of contract;
- a breach of a representation will not enable a breach of contract claim, but may, however, lead to a misrepresentation that makes the contract voidable.

An action under misrepresentation is available if the untrue representation is considered 'actionable' (see Fig 3.1). This means there is a legal remedy available where a false statement

Figure 3.1 The required elements of actionable misrepresentation

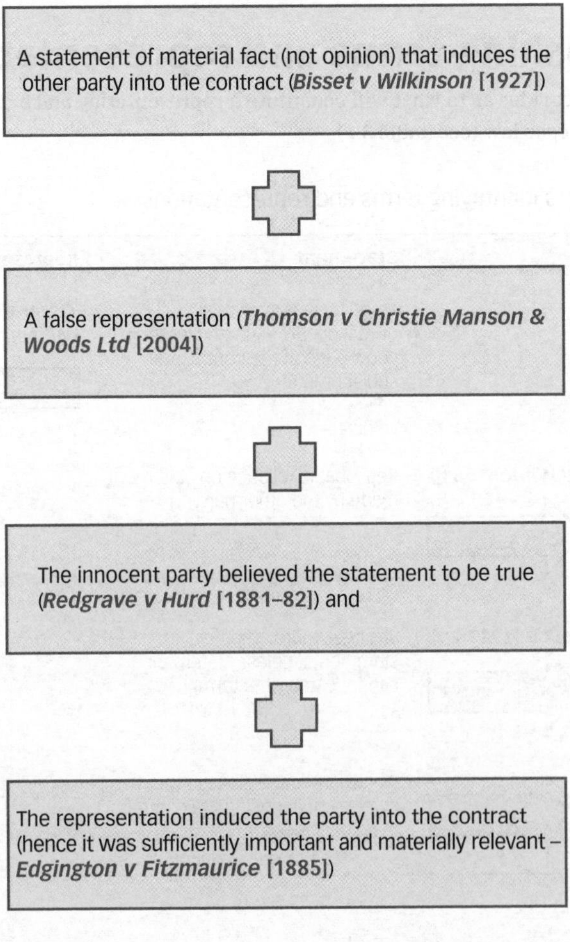

A statement of material fact (not opinion) that induces the other party into the contract (*Bisset v Wilkinson* [1927])

A false representation (*Thomson v Christie Manson & Woods Ltd* [2004])

The innocent party believed the statement to be true (*Redgrave v Hurd* [1881–82]) and

The representation induced the party into the contract (hence it was sufficiently important and materially relevant – *Edgington v Fitzmaurice* [1885])

of fact (not opinion—*Smith v Land & House Property Corp* [1884]) is made that induces the other party to enter the contract.

Silence as misrepresentation

The general rule of contract is that silence cannot amount to a misrepresentation. Naturally, there are exceptions:

1. If there is a material change in the circumstances.

Revision tip

Questions can often appear on this issue where a party has not volunteered information between the agreement of a sale, for example, and the conclusion of the contract. The cases of *With v O'Flanagan* [1936] and *Spice Girls v Aprilia World Service BV* [2002] provide good authority for examples of material changes amounting to misrepresentation.

2. If remaining silent would make a statement misleading.

Where a person is asked a question during the negotiations, and an answer is offered (although there is no legal duty to answer questions here), there is an obligation that the answer is truthful, full, and complete. This is an interesting aspect of the law as a true statement, but one that misleads the other party, can still amount to a misrepresentation.

Nottingham Patent Brick & Tile Co Ltd v Butler (1886) 16 QBD 778

A solicitor was asked about the existence of restrictive covenants on land and replied that he was unaware of any. However, whilst strictly true, this was because the solicitor had not inspected the deeds. This silence was held to be a misrepresentation.

3. If the parties had a fiduciary relationship.

Where a fiduciary relationship exists it is presumed that any material fact must be revealed to the other party and if this is not volunteered, then the silence can be held to be a misrepresentation.

4. In cases where the contract is one of good faith (eg insurance contracts).

Certain contracts, such as contracts of insurance, require *uberrimae fidei*—'utmost good faith'. This requires full disclosure of relevant factors that would influence a decision to enter an agreement or not (*Lambert v Co-op Insurance Society Ltd* [1975]).

If one of the four listed exceptions is present, an actionable misrepresentation is possible.

Types of misrepresentation

The three types of actionable misrepresentation are:

Fraudulent misrepresentation

This involves a false statement that has been made knowingly or recklessly (*Derry v Peek* [1889]). This entitles the innocent party to claim rescission of the contract and/or damages, and sue in the tort of deceit.

> *Revision tip*
>
> Note that whilst claims may be made for fraudulent misrepresentation, fraud in this instance is closer to the criminal law than civil liability. There may be problems inherent in establishing sufficient evidence to sustain an allegation of fraud, and hence many claimants attempt to seek a remedy under negligent misrepresentation (see *Royscot Trust Ltd v Rogerson* [1991] and *Long v Lloyd* [1958] for examples of the difficulty in proving fraudulent misrepresentation).

Negligent misrepresentation

This involves a false statement being made which induces the other party to enter a contract. However, it does not involve fraud, and so is easier to prove, as the party making the statement is unlikely to be able to demonstrate that they believed the statement to be true, or held a reasonable belief that it was true. This entitles the innocent party to claim rescission and damages.

> *Revision tip*
>
> As the **Misrepresentation Act 1967 s 2(1)** provides a remedy for negligent misrepresentation, and the courts have held that this calculation should be made in the same way as for those awarded in cases of fraud, a claim for misrepresentation may actually provide the claimant with a 'better' monetary damages award than if a claim of breach of contract had been made.

Innocent misrepresentation

This involves a false statement being made but in the honest, albeit mistaken, belief that it was true. This party needs to establish that they believed in the truthfulness of the statement made, and they had reasonable grounds upon which to hold this belief. This entitles the innocent party to claim rescission as the contract is voidable and, if this is not possible, it may provide for a damages claim in lieu of rescission under the **Misrepresentation Act 1967 s 2(2)**.

Revision tip

Note a key distinction between negligent misrepresentation (**Misrepresentation Act 1967 s 2(1)**) and innocent misrepresentation. The party who claims misrepresentation has the burden of demonstrating that an actionable misrepresentation has taken place. An action under the **Misrepresentation Act 1967 s 2(1)** will shift the burden of proof onto the party who made the misrepresentation to demonstrate that they had reasonable grounds for believing the facts as represented to be true. If they demonstrate this then the misrepresentation will be wholly innocent, whilst if they fail in this task it will amount to a negligent misrepresentation.

Remedies for misrepresentation

The remedies available depend upon the type of misrepresentation involved (fraudulent, negligent, or innocent).

Rescission

The remedy of rescission is an equitable remedy where the party has the option to have the contract avoided and the parties are returned to their pre-contractual position.

Damages

A simpler method of remedying the loss sustained due to a misrepresentation is through an award of damages.

In the case of fraudulent misrepresentation, the damages are intended to place the party in the position they would have been if the fraud had not been committed.

Damages can be awarded in contract and tort (such as fraud) and, of course, through statute.

For those who have been subject to an innocent misrepresentation, the courts have been provided the discretion to award damages under the **Misrepresentation Act 1967 s 2(2)** in place of rescission. Damages are rarely awarded under this section, and when they are, the assessment is based on the contractual remedy of damages that seeks to place the parties in the position they would have been in had the representation not been untrue.

Duress

Freedom of contract relies on the presumption that those who enter into contracts do so under their own free will. If a contract is established on the basis of violence (or a threat), or unlawful economic pressure, this may be considered to be a case of duress. For duress to succeed there must be 'overbearing of the will'.

Duress makes the contract voidable at common law.

Duress

****

Economic duress

It is vital to distinguish between (1) economic duress and (2) strong pressure in commercial dealings. The first is actionable and the second may be considered good business practice.

The following may provide guidance as to where economic pressure amounts to duress:

- illegitimate pressure (which need not be unlawful—*R v Attorney-General for England and Wales* [2003]), such as exerting unacceptable levels of pressure which go beyond those normally expected in commercial negotiations;
- whether the party claiming duress demonstrated protestations against the contract; and
- whether the party had any alternative to proceeding with the contract, evidenced by the availability of independent advice that could have better informed the claimant (*Atlas Express Ltd v Kafco Importers & Distributors* [1989]).

See *The Atlantic Baron (North Ocean Shipping v Hyundai Construction)* [1979].

Undue influence

Where undue influence has been used to form the contract, it will be voidable. This generally occurs when an individual's vulnerabilities are subjugated.

To gain protection from the doctrine, the claimant has to demonstrate that:

- they would not have entered into the contract except for the undue influence; and
- they had placed trust and confidence in the other party.

Restriction of rescission

Undue influence is based on equity, and as such the courts may use equitable remedies to prevent an unjust outcome, such as to rescind the contract. However, being an equitable remedy, it is a remedy that is provided at the discretion of the court, and the right to rescission may be lost if:

- the party is deemed to have affirmed the contract (such as not making any outward sign of protest against the contract);
- they unduly delay in seeking to rescind; or
- the contract involved property which has been sold on before the complainant brought their claim.

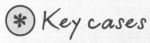 Key cases

Case	Facts	Principle
Bell v Lever Bros Ltd [1932] AC 161 (HL)	A company employee was dismissed and provided with a redundancy payment, but he had previously breached the contract which would have allowed for early termination with no compensation. In an action for recovery of the sum, it was held this mistake was not void as to quality.	The mistake in the agreement was not sufficiently different from the agreement which the parties had in their contemplation (it was not a fundamental mistake) and there was no misrepresentation.
Great Peace Shipping Ltd v Tsavliris Salvage International Ltd [2002] EWCA Civ 1407	In the rescue of a vessel at sea, a ship was hired to assist under a contract for a minimum of a five-day period. This was due to the belief that the ships were in close proximity, whilst they were actually 400 miles apart. Another vessel was discovered to be closer and a contract was entered into for this vessel, with an attempt to have the first contract held void on the basis of common mistake.	It was held that there is no basis on which a contract is to be rescinded due to mutual mistake where, at common law, the contract is valid and enforceable. Hence, mistakes as to quality cannot make the contract voidable in equity.
Nottingham Patent Brick & Tile Co Ltd v Butler [1886] 16 QBD 778	The defendant's solicitor was asked if he was aware of a restrictive covenant on land the claimant was to purchase. He said he was unaware of such a covenant. Whilst true, this was because he had not looked at the property deeds.	Whilst a person may not be obliged to answer questions put to them, where one is offered, there is an obligation that the answer is truthful, full, and complete. Hence a true statement, but one that misleads the other party, may still amount to a misrepresentation.
Shogun Finance Ltd v Hudson [2003] UKHL 62	Hudson purchased a used Mitsubishi motorcar in good faith from a rogue, the rogue having obtained the car through a hire-purchase agreement with Shogun Finance Ltd. The rogue had impersonated a man who had no knowledge or involvement with the fraud. The court had to determine which of the previous authorities (on fraudulent activities and mistake as to the identity of the party) was effective.	The Lords held by a majority of 3:2 that the rogue did not obtain a good title that could be passed on to another. The two dissenting Lords wished to reverse the decision of *Cundy* so that a contract had been formed, but the law in *Cundy* remained good. Here, the finance company believed it was dealing, and only would deal, with the person who the rogue had impersonated. It had performed adequate checks to verify the information presented and as such the contract between the rogue and the finance company was void. This meant the innocent third party lost their purchase price and the vehicle.

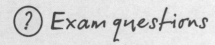

? Exam questions

Problem question

Cal owns a poodle which he has decided to sell as he is moving into an apartment that does not allow residents to keep animals in the property. Malik is very interested in purchasing the dog for his young son Quentin and arranges to inspect it. Cal informs Malik that the dog is very friendly and has a pleasant demeanour—especially around children. Cal also states that the dog is a pure breed, which therefore makes it valuable. However, Cal did not inform Malik that the poodle, whilst being very friendly, is scared of balloons and reacts aggressively to anyone holding them.

Malik decides to purchase the dog. Malik presents the dog to Quentin at his birthday party, where children are making noise and some, including Quentin, are holding balloons. The dog slips away from his lead and attacks two of the children who subsequently require medical treatment.

The poodle runs away from the scene and Malik is subsequently contacted by the local authority which has found the dog roaming around the town and taken it into its possession until Malik collects it. When Malik collects the dog he is informed that it is not a pure breed.

Advise Malik on the civil issues (including possible remedies) surrounding this case.

An outline answer is included at the end of the book.

Essay question

Describe how the common law has developed tests to differentiate between terms and representations, and critically assess their effectiveness.

To see an outline answer to this question visit www.oup.com/lawrevision/

#4

Contract III: contractual terms and statutory protection

Key facts

- The parties to a contract may express terms and/or terms may be implied. The sources and effects of implied terms are essential to the rights of the parties and obligations imposed on them.

- Terms can be implied through the courts, through customs, and from statute.

- Terms are identified as conditions, warranties, or innominate—this distinction is relevant when identifying the remedies for breach.

- Statutes regulate the rights and obligations applicable to consumers and traders.

Changes to statutory protection

From 1 October 2015 the **Consumer Rights Act (CRA)** came into effect and has changed the statutory sources of protection in business-to-consumer (B2C) contracts, and to business-to-business (B2B) contracts (albeit to a lesser extent in this second category of contractual relationships).

The **CRA 2015** formed part of the government's initiative to reform consumer rights, in some instances simplifying the current range of legislation, and in other areas seeking to codify and establish a consistent application of the law.

The CRA is comprised of three parts:

- Part 1 is concerned with consumer contracts for goods, digital content, and services;
- Part 2 deals with unfair terms; and
- Part 3 considers miscellaneous provisions such as investigatory powers, enforcement mechanisms and collective redress, and other private actions relating to anti–competitive behaviour in competition law.

Contractual terms

Having identified that a contract exists, it is necessary to consider the terms of the contract. Contract terms are essential in defining the obligations of the parties and determining when the contract has been broken and the result of that breach. When interpreting contractual provisions the courts will generally adopt a commercial common sense perspective to the agreement as a whole, not restricting itself to reference to the provision of the contract in dispute. However, and particularly in relation to contracts established between sophisticated parties such as big businesses, the courts should be less willing to depart from a literal reading of the contractual terms and their nuances (see *Wood v Capita Insurance Services Limited* [2017]).

Terms of the contract, differentiating between conditions and warranties, the use and validity of exclusion clauses, and the various statutory implied terms in consumer contracts are common examination questions. Knowledge and application of case law and statute is essential in this area.

Express terms

Express terms are, naturally, those that have been expressed by the parties in some form— written (eg in an employment law context, in a works handbook); or they may be identified from the oral negotiations between the parties.

Implied terms

Terms are implied into contracts by the courts, through customs, and through statutes. They establish the obligations on the parties and their rights under the contract. By their nature, implied terms are not expressed orally or in writing.

Terms implied by the courts

Courts imply terms into a contract as a matter of fact or a matter of law:

- 'As a matter of fact': are undertaken to help make sense of the contract at hand, or to make the contract work.

- 'As a matter of law': are applied to a particular type or class of contracts in general and so the impact is potentially far more significant (*Liverpool CC v Irwin* [1977]).

Revision tip

Remember that whilst the courts may be willing to imply terms, they will not re-write a poorly drafted contract. See *Wells v Devani* [2016] where the Court of Appeal explained 'it is wrong in principle to turn an incomplete bargain into a legally binding contract by adding expressly agreed terms and implied terms together'. The parties should ensure that important contract terms have been agreed even if the complete contract has yet to be ascertained.

There are two main reasons for the courts implying terms as a matter of fact:

- **business efficacy**: the court is implying a term merely to make commercial sense of the transaction (*The Moorcock* [1886–90]); or

- because the term was so obvious that each party must have assumed it would be included ('the officious bystander test'—*Shirlaw v Southern Foundries* [1939]).

The intention of both of these tests is to make the contract reflect the manifestly presumed intentions of the parties—but no more than that. It is not an exercise in re-writing the contract just because one of the parties would like to do so.

The Supreme Court considered when a term is to be implied into a contract and reviewed the previous authority provided by the Privy Council in *Attorney General of Belize v Belize Telecom Ltd* [2009]. The Supreme Court considered that *Belize* was an 'inspired discussion rather than authoritative guidance on the law of implied terms'. In *Marks and Spencer plc v BNP Paribas Securities Services Trust Company (Jersey) Limited and another* [2015] it affirmed that (here) a term will only be implied where it is needed for business efficacy; it is insufficient to include it simply because the parties would have agreed to the term (had it been put to them). Therefore, the Supreme Court decided to reject implying a term as it considered the term was not crucial in order to make the contract practicable.

Terms implied through customs

The courts can imply local customs (eg in *Smith v Wilson* [1832] the court implied the local custom that '1,000 rabbits' actually meant '1,200 rabbits').

The courts will look towards the custom being notorious, certain, commonplace, reasonable, and legal to comprise an implied term. The term may also be implied on the basis of the previous dealings between the parties (*Spurling J Ltd v Bradshaw* [1956]).

Terms implied through statutes

Protection of consumers and those entering contracts has been significantly enhanced through the actions of Parliament. The **Sale of Goods Act (SOGA) 1979** (now replaced in consumer contracts by the **CRA 2015**), for example, has been particularly prominent in this area.

Types of terms

Defining the type of term is important to appreciate the remedy available to the innocent party upon breach (see Fig 4.1).

Revision tip

It is important to remember that the courts may imply terms because the contract is silent on the particular issue but where an express clause is included a contradictory term will not be implied (unless required by law).

When answering a question as to a breach of contract, you will have to identify which 'type' of term it is—condition or warranty. The reason is simply because of the remedy available to the innocent party. However, always note that any breach of contract entitles the innocent party to claim damages.

Revision tip

The identification of terms as conditions or warranties is generally assessed as to the importance attached to the term by the parties at the time of contracting.

Figure 4.1 Types of Term

A term
is either a

	Warranty	Condition
	Damages	Damages
Remedies for breach	Must continue with the contract	May choose to end the contract or may choose to affirm it

What about innominate terms?

Still just a warranty or a condition – simply cannot be identified in advance. The results of the breach of the contract will allow the court to identify which type of term it is

Warranty

A warranty is a lesser term of a contract and the innocent party may seek the remedy of damages for a breach, but they are not entitled to end (repudiate) the contract (*Bettini v Gye* (1876)).

Condition

A condition is an important term of the contract often described as going to the 'heart of the contract' or is 'what the contract is all about' (*Poussard v Spiers* [1876]).

A breach of a condition enables the injured party to bring the contract to an end *and* claim damages. If the contract is to be ended this must be acted upon quickly and within a reasonable time.

Revision tip

Simply because the word 'condition' is used in a contract will not oblige the court to interpret it as such (*L Schuler AG v Wickman Machine Tool Sales* [1974]). However, this does not prevent a party from identifying a term that they consider essential and insisting that it is a condition (*Lombard North Central Plc v Butterworth* [1987]). Where statute has implied 'conditions' into contracts, these will be interpreted as such (eg **SOGA 1979**).

Innominate/intermediate terms

An innominate term is one not yet defined. Courts may adopt a 'term-based' approach in identifying a condition from a warranty, but sometimes it is more appropriate to look to a 'breach-based' approach—looking at how serious the consequences of the breach were. Essentially this approach works backwards—identifying the breach and its consequences, which will then determine if the term is a condition (a serious breach) or warranty (a lesser breach).

Innominate terms have *not* replaced conditions or warranties; what the courts look to is whether the innocent party has been deprived of substantially the whole benefit of the contract. If they have, then the term breached will be held a condition; if not, then the term will be held a warranty (*Hongkong Fir Shipping Co v Kawasaki Kisen Kaisha* [1962]).

✅ *Looking for extra marks?*

The courts have stated that if there is an established commercial practice regarding the status of terms used in commercial contracts, these should be interpreted accordingly to ensure certainty between the parties (*Bunge Corp v Tradax* [1981]).

The Unfair Contract Terms Act 1977

- UCTA 1977 ensures that certain exclusion clauses are removed or held invalid by the courts.
- UCTA 1977 regulates the use of non-contractual notices attempting to restrict liability for negligence.
- Certain exclusion clauses will automatically be considered void under the Act (such as excluding liability for death or personal injury due to negligence) and those remaining have to satisfy the test of 'reasonableness'.
- UCTA 1977 is concerned with business liability in contract and tort, and hence the liability for breach of obligations or duties relating to that person's trade, business, craft, or profession.

Liability in negligence

UCTA 1977 specifically voids attempts through contractual terms/notices to exclude liability for death or personal injury caused through negligence (s 2(1)). CRA 2015 s 65 provides similar protection for consumers.

Reasonableness

UCTA 1977 contains provision for how the reasonableness or otherwise of an exclusion clause will be determined.

✅ Looking for extra marks?

Reasonableness is determined through s 11 but note its somewhat harsh application to businesses. For example, *Watford Electronic Ltd v Sanderson CFL Ltd* [2001] demonstrated that an otherwise unreasonable limitation clause would be allowed unless the term is so unreasonable that the court must move to restrict it. In this case, involving the supply of computer equipment, a clause limited liability to £104,596, and this was considered reasonable even though the actual losses sustained were £5.5 million.

The obligation to demonstrate that the clause is reasonable rests with the party relying on the clause.

The House of Lords offered assistance for determining reasonableness of an exclusion clause in *Smith v Eric S Bush* [1990] based on the following factors:

- whether the parties were of equal bargaining power;
- in situations involving advice, whether it was practicable (in costs and time) to obtain alternative advice;

- the level of complexity and difficulty in the task which was subject to the exclusion of liability; and
- which of the parties was better able to bear any losses and whether insurance should have been sought.

In *Goodlife Foods Ltd v Hall Fire Protection Ltd* [2018] the defective installation of a fire suppression system led to losses by the claimant of over £6 million. A clause in the standard terms of the supplier's contract excluded liability for any losses (unless additional insurance protection was purchased—which was not). The Court of Appeal held the clause to be effective and had been incorporated correctly. This was despite the exclusion clause being wide and excluded liability for damages 'directly or indirectly resulting from our negligence or delay or failure or malfunction of the systems or components provided by HFS for whatsoever reason'. The nature of the clause was not unusual nor was it onerous. It had not been 'buried' in small print within the contract. The parties were also of equal bargaining positions and, very importantly, the claimants could have gone elsewhere and found an alternative supplier who did not include the exclusion clause in the contract.

Liability under misrepresentation

UCTA 1977 s 8 replaced s 3 of the Misrepresentation Act 1967 and prohibits any term in a contract that purports to restrict or exclude a liability for a misrepresentation made before the contract was agreed; or attempts to restrict or exclude a remedy the other party would have in the event of such a misrepresentation. This is unless the party seeking to rely on the clause can demonstrate its reasonableness under UCTA 1977 s 1(1).

The Consumer Rights Act 2015

CRA 2015 revoked the Unfair Terms in Consumer Contracts Regulations 1999 (UTCCR) and established, among other requirements, that contract terms and notices are fair (s 62) and will therefore be binding on the consumer. This does not prevent the consumer from seeking to rely on the term or the notice if he or she chooses to do so.

Fairness

A term or notice will be held to be unfair if, contrary to the requirement of good faith, it causes significant imbalance in the parties' rights and obligations under the contract, and this is to the detriment of the consumer. Fairness is determined by taking into account the nature of the subject matter of the contract; by reference to all the circumstances existing when the contract was agreed; and to all of the other terms of the contract or of any other contract on which it depends.

It is important to note that where the term is void because it relates to the purported exclusion of liability in: (a) goods contracts (s 31), (b) digital content contracts (s 47),

(c) services contracts (s 57), or (d) exclusion of negligence liability (s 65), the terms will remain void regardless of any fairness test.

Exclusion from assessment of fairness

Section 64 identifies that a term of a consumer contract may not be assessed for fairness under s 62 to the extent that it (a) specifies the main subject matter of the contract, or (b) the assessment is of the appropriateness of the price payable. However, this part of s 64 excludes the term from assessment only if it is transparent and prominent. For example, the price paid for a holiday by a consumer would not be subject to a fairness test where this price is transparent and prominent. But it is quite possible that in 'the small print' terms are incorporated relating to cancellation charges or other miscellaneous prices. These would be susceptible to the fairness scrutiny (thus replacing reg 6(2) UTCCR).

A term is transparent for the purposes of this Part if it is expressed in plain and intelligible language and (in the case of a written term) is legible.

A term is prominent for the purposes of this section if it is brought to the consumer's attention in such a way that an average consumer would be aware of the term.

Revision tip

As the **CRA 2015** is intended to provide protection to consumers **s 71** operates so that in proceedings before a court which relate to a term of a consumer contract, the court has an obligation to consider its fairness. This applies even if neither party to the proceedings has raised that issue or indicated that it intends to raise it.

Enforcement

Where a term/notice is deemed to be unfair, it is not binding on the consumer (s 62(1) and (2)) but, where possible, the contract will continue without that term. On the basis that unfair terms have been used in a consumer contract, the Competition and Markets Authority, along with other regulators, have enforcement functions conferred on them. Schedule 5 outlines the investigatory powers of the regulators. Following a finding of use of an unfair term, the regulator may apply to a court for an injunction to restrain further use of the unfair term. The regulator may also collate and make public (where appropriate) actions taken against such (rogue) traders.

The sale of goods and consumer contracts for goods

For protection through SOGA 1979 and CRA 2015, a sale must take place (s 2(1) SOGA and s 5 CRA 2015). Therefore barters (exchanging items) and loans are not protected unless a transfer of the ownership has occurred (although the parties to the barter are protected through the **Supply of Goods and Services Act 1982**).

Goods are defined as 'all personal chattels other than things in action and money' (s 61(1)). In B2C contracts 'goods' means any tangible moveable items—including water, gas, and electricity if and only if they are put up for supply in a limited volume or set quantity (s 2(8)). In *Computer Associates UK Ltd v The Software Incubator Ltd* [2018] the supply of software (here it was a download) was not 'goods.' Goods must be in a tangible form (eg on a disk) for the purposes of legislation such as the **Commercial Agents (Council Directive) Regulations 1993** to be considered to amount to a 'sale of goods'.

The following are the major protections implied into contracts through SOGA 1979 (with B2C protection afforded similarly through CRA 2015):

Section 12—title to goods

The buyer is then able to enjoy 'quiet possession of the goods'. In order to achieve this, the first party must possess the title to transfer or have the owner's consent to dispose of the good (*Rowland v Divall* [1923]). If, however, the transfer of ownership is 'voidable' then SOGA 1979 s 23 is important and should be considered in light of the transfer of title and in situations of misrepresentation.

Section 13—description of goods

Goods that are sold by description (the description must have been relied on) must correspond to that description (B2C contracts see s 11 CRA 2015).

Protection is lost where the buyer has taken the responsibility for verifying the good themselves (*Harlingdon and Leinster Enterprises v Christopher Hull Fine Art* [1990]).

The protection of s 13 also applies to advertisements and sales materials where the buyer has relied on the information.

✅ *Looking for extra marks?*

It is important to note that whilst the sections of the Act are separated, they may work independently of each other or in unison. For example, s 13 is not concerned with the quality of the product, which may be perfectly fine in terms of its quality and fitness for purpose, but not as described. This would still allow a remedy under **SOGA 1979** (*Arcos v Ronaasen* [1933]). In *Beale v Taylor* [1967] the Court of Appeal held that where a private seller sold a car that was described as a Triumph Herald, but in reality was two cars welded together (with only one half of the car corresponding to the description), whilst the buyer could not rely on s 14 as to the car's quality, an action was permitted under s 13 (as it applies to all sales).

Section 14(2)—quality of goods

Section 14(2) incorporates a term in sales established in the course of business requiring the goods to be of a satisfactory quality (B2C contracts see s 9 CRA 2015). 'Quality' will vary between products depending on issues such as whether the good was brand new or used but is assessed on the basis of the reasonable person's understanding of quality in the particular case.

Features to be considered when assessing the quality of a good include:

- fitness for all the purposes for which goods of the kind in question are commonly supplied;
- appearance and finish;
- freedom from minor defects;
- safety; and
- durability.

There are limitations to the protection afforded and it will not apply where:

- defects were pointed out to the buyer before the contract was made (*Bartlett v Sidney Marcus Ltd* [1965]);
- the buyer has examined the goods before contracting and the defects were obvious (although any other defects are still covered)—s 14(2C)(b);
- a business sells anything (eg a fishing boat)—it does so in the course of its business—see *Stevenson v Rogers* [1999].

> ### ✅ *Looking for extra marks?*
> The main value of **s 14(2)** is that the liability is strict. This means that regardless of how the defect in the good was created (remember many businesses simply re-sell goods and hence are not responsible for manufacturing defects present in the good), if there is a defect, protection is granted under **s 14(2)** against the seller (not the manufacturer).

Section 14 (3)—fitness for purpose

Goods must be reasonably fit for the buyer's specified purpose (B2C contracts see s **10 CRA 2015**). The buyer can gain protection from either implicit or explicit reliance as to quality.

The buyer must express (*Ashington Piggeries Ltd v Christopher Hill Ltd* [1971]) or imply (*Grant v Australian Knitting Mills Ltd* [1936]) the purpose for which they are buying the good to engage this section. Providing the buyer makes clear their purpose, it does not matter that the goods might not normally be sold for that purpose. The seller will not be held liable when the customer's individual peculiarities make the good unfit for purpose (*Griffiths v Peter Conway* [1939]).

Section 15—sale by sample

If a sale of goods takes place through a sample of a larger consignment, the bulk of the consignment must correspond to the sample (in practical terms, this section is of most use to businesses but for B2C contracts see s 13 CRA 2015). This means that if the sample is of a good quality, the buyer can expect the remaining items to be of a similar standard. This also works in reverse—where the sample is of a poor standard the bulk can be considered as being similarly poor. CRA 2015 also provides consumers protection in a contract to supply goods by reference to a model of the goods that is seen or examined by the consumer before entering into the contract. A term is implied to the effect that the goods will match the model. An exception is provided to the extent that any differences between the model and the goods are brought to the consumer's attention before the consumer enters into the contract (s 14).

The goods should also be free from defects that would make their quality unsatisfactory—which would not have been apparent on a reasonable inspection (*Godley v Perry* [1960]).

Application of the Act

Protection under SOGA 1979 requires the buyer to act within a reasonable time to enforce the rights associated with a condition. After this reasonable time, the term will be considered a warranty and the buyer will not be able to repudiate the contract, but they may seek damages/repair or replacement of the goods.

Buyer's remedies for breach
Right to reject goods

Rejection is permissible where the seller has breached a condition.

The injured party can reject the goods and refuse to pay the sum agreed, or to claim for any money paid.

In order to reject the goods, s 35 lays down a requirement for quick action and any delay may result in the buyer losing the right (this is dependent on the facts of the case—*Rogers v Parish* [1987]). An unreasonably delayed rejection will prevent the buyer from rejecting the good (*Jones v Gallagher and Gallagher* [2005]).

Right to claim damages

Under SOGA 1979, the right for damages usually involves the non-delivery of goods where there is a difference in price between the cost of the goods at the time of the contract, and the cost when the good has not been supplied. Damages are designed to place the injured party, as far as possible, in the position in which they should have been before the breach. See Fig 4.2 for consumer contracts prior to 1 October 2015.

Seller's remedies for breach

The seller has remedies in the event of a breach by the buyer—such as where the buyer refuses to pay for the goods ordered or if they refuse to accept the supply of the goods.

Consumer's rights to enforce terms about goods (s 19 CRA 2015)

****

Figure 4.2 SOGA 1979 consequences of breach (particularly for consumer contracts prior to 1 October 2015)

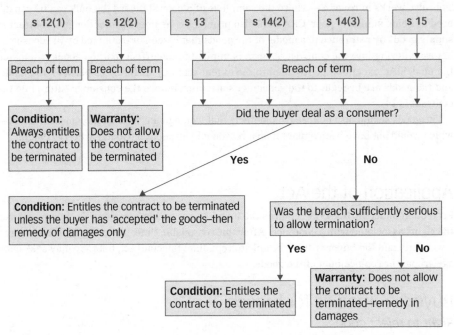

These rights are typically used when the seller is selling the goods to another business and the buyer becomes insolvent—therefore it is unable to pay for the goods:

- the seller may retain possession of the goods until payment has been made, unless the seller waives the right or the price is paid;

- the seller may stop the goods in transit and therefore restrict the physical passing of the goods to the buyer (where the buyer is insolvent); and

- the seller may re-sell the goods to another buyer to mitigate any potential losses (where the goods are perishable or the seller has notified the buyer of the intention to sell if payment is not received).

Consumer's rights to enforce terms about goods (s 19 CRA 2015)

The protection afforded to B2B contracts through implied terms is similar in many respects to those terms guaranteed in B2C contracts. Existing/previous legislation sought to categorize contractual terms as either conditions (which go to the heart of the contract) or warranties

Table 4.1 CRA 2015 rights and remedies

The right	Available remedy
Section 9 (goods to be of satisfactory quality) Section 10 (goods to be fit for particular purpose) Section 11 (goods to be as described) Section 13 (goods to match a sample) Section 14 (goods to match a model seen or examined) Section 16 (goods not conforming to contract if digital content does not conform)	(a) the short-term right to reject (**ss 20 and 22**); (b) the right to repair or replacement (**s 23**); and (c) the right to a price reduction or the final right to reject (**ss 20 and 24**).
Section 12 (other pre-contract information included in contract)	The consumer has the right to recover from the trader the amount of any costs incurred by them as a result of the breach, up to the amount of the price paid or the value of other consideration given for the goods.
Section 15 (installation as part of conformity of goods with contract)	(a) the right to repair or replacement (**s 23**); and (b) the right to a price reduction or the final right to reject (**ss 20 and 24**).
Section 17 (trader to have right to supply the goods etc.)	The consumer has a right to reject (subject to **s 20**).

(lesser terms), breach of which determined whether the consumer could reject the contract (a right only allowed for breach of a condition) or to affirm the contract and seek damages. There was some distinction between the remedies for breach of the terms depending on the legislative instrument which provided the right (see Table 4.1). As such, the **CRA 2015** seeks to add consistency to the approach of remedies.

Right to reject (s 20)

The right of rejection is exercised if the consumer indicates to the trader that they are rejecting the goods and treating the contract as at an end. This indication may be something the consumer says or does, but it must be sufficiently clear to be understood by the trader.

Once the right to reject has been invoked, the trader has a duty to give the consumer a refund, and the consumer has a duty to make the goods available for collection by the trader or (if there is an agreement for the consumer to return rejected goods) to return them as agreed. Regardless of whether or not the consumer has a duty to return the rejected goods, the trader must bear any reasonable costs of returning them, other than any costs incurred by the consumer in returning the goods in person to the place where the consumer took physical possession.

Time limit for short-term right to reject (s 22)

A consumer who has the short-term right to reject loses it where this is not exercised according to the limits outlined below (unless the trader and the consumer agree that it may be exercised later—which must not be a shorter timeframe than the minimum established in law).

The short-term right to reject is the end of 30 days, beginning with the first day after these have all happened:

(a) ownership or (in the case of a contract for the hire of goods, a hire-purchase agreement, or a conditional sales contract) possession of the goods has been transferred to the consumer;

(b) the goods have been delivered; and

(c) where the contract requires the trader to install the goods or take other action to enable the consumer to use them, the trader has notified the consumer that the action has been taken.

REMEMBER: In the event that the goods are of a kind that can reasonably be expected to perish after a shorter period than the right to reject above would give, the time limit for exercising the short-term right to reject is the end of that shorter period.

Where the consumer requests or agrees to the repair or replacement of goods, the periods outlined above stop running for the length of the waiting period.

Right to repair or replacement (s 23)

Where the right to repair (making the goods conform to the required standard) or replacement of the goods applies, and where the consumer requires the trader to perform this task, the trader must:

(a) do so within a reasonable time and without significant inconvenience to the consumer; and

(b) bear any necessary costs incurred in doing so (including in particular the cost of any labour, materials, or postage).

The consumer cannot require the trader to repair or replace the goods if that remedy is impossible, or is disproportionate compared to the other of those remedies. 'Disproportionate' involves the imposition of costs on the trader which, compared to those imposed by the other remedies, are unreasonable, taking into account:

(a) the value which the goods would have if they conformed to the contract;

(b) the significance of the lack of conformity; and

(c) whether the other remedy could be effected without significant inconvenience to the consumer.

Questions as to what is a reasonable time or significant inconvenience are to be determined taking account of the nature of the goods, and the purpose for which the goods were acquired.

The Supply of Goods and Services Act 1982

The legislation governs the supply of services, and the supply of faulty goods and materials provided with the services in B2B contracts. It requires that a supplier of a service, acting in the course of business, provides:

- that service with reasonable skill and care;
- within a 'reasonable' time (unless there is an express agreement to the contrary); and
- to make a reasonable charge for the service.

Part I of the Act provides protection by implying terms into contracts involving the transfer of property in goods, and into contracts for the hire of goods. The Act complements the rights provided in SOGA 1979.

Transfer of property in goods

This includes any contract where the title to the goods passes to another, and is not a contract for the sale of goods, or contracts under hire-purchase agreements (as other statutes offer protection). An example of such a contract would be for a boiler to be installed in a launderette.

The Act gives the protections outlined in Table 4.2 (particularly relevant for consumer contracts prior to 1 October 2015).

Contract of hire

The title to the goods is not passed (transferred) to the other party, but a temporary possession is provided.

The Act gives the protections outlined in Table 4.3 (particularly for consumer contracts prior to 1 October 2015).

Table 4.2 Transfer of goods: classification of protective rights

Protection	Condition or warranty
The right to transfer the property (**s 2(1)**)	A condition
Quiet possession and freedom from encumbrances (**s 2(2)**)	A warranty
Correspondence with description (**s 3(2)**)	A condition if the buyer deals as a consumer
Satisfactory quality (**s 4(2)**)	A condition if the buyer deals as a consumer
Fitness for purpose (**s 4(5)**)	A condition if the buyer deals as a consumer
Correspondence with sample (**s 5(2)**)	A condition if the buyer deals as a consumer

Consumer contracts for services

****

Table 4.3 Hire of goods: classification of protective rights

Protection	Condition or warranty
Right to hire (**s 7(1)**)	A condition
Quiet possession and freedom from encumbrances (**s 7(2)**)	A warranty
Correspondence with description (**s 8(2)**)	A condition if the buyer deals as a consumer
Satisfactory quality (**s 9(2)**)	A condition if the buyer deals as a consumer
Fitness for purpose (**s 9(5)**)	A condition if the buyer deals as a consumer
Correspondence with sample (**s 10(2)**)	A condition if the buyer deals as a consumer

Supply of a service

Part II of the Act covers the very important protections afforded where a service is supplied. These terms are implied into contracts and are not included in **SOGA 1979**.

Section 13—duty to exercise reasonable care and skill

(Where the supplier is acting in the course of business.) The protection is different from the implied term as to quality in **SOGA 1979 s 14** which imposes a **strict liability** standard, in that the test as to reasonable care and skill is based on the test established in tort law.

Section 14—performance within a reasonable time

Where a time for the service to be carried out and/or completed is not identified in the contract, s **14** provides that this must be achieved within a 'reasonable' time. What is reasonable is for the courts to decide when investigating the facts of each case.

Section 15—obligation to pay a reasonable price

Regardless of whether the supplier is acting in the course of business or not, there is an implied term of a reasonable price to be paid. The section is not implied where the price has already been agreed in the contract, or has been agreed between the parties in the course of their dealings with each other. **Section 15(2)** states that a reasonable price is to be determined on the facts of the case.

Consumer contracts for services

The **CRA 2015** guarantees various terms into contracts for the supply of a service. The main provisions are included in ss **49–52** which provide:

Service to be performed with reasonable care and skill (s 49)

Every contract to supply a service is to be treated as including a term that the trader must perform the service with reasonable care and skill. This, consequently, no longer requires such a term to be referred to as being 'implied' into the contract. Further, the CRA does not provide a definition for 'care and skill' although it will likely follow that used in the previous applicable legislation (the **Supply of Goods and Services Act 1982 s 13**) and case law identifying that this will differ between industries, and be 'reasonable' will also be a variable concept, determined presumably with reference to the price paid for the service. The available remedies are included in Table 4.4.

Information about the trader or service to be binding (s 50)

Every contract to supply a service is to be treated as including, as a term of the contract, anything that is said or written to the consumer, by or on behalf of the trader, about the trader or the service. This becomes effective where the information is taken into account by the consumer when deciding to enter into the contract, or where it is taken into account by the consumer when making any decision about the service after entering into the contract.

This is an entirely new provision in the legislation (not previously incorporated in the **Supply of Goods and Services Act 1982**) and operates where promises/statements are made by a trader or on their behalf which induce the consumer to enter into the contract.

Further, given the **Consumer Contracts (Information, Cancellation and Additional Charges) Regulations 2013** and the requirement imposed on traders to supply certain information to consumers, where such information is provided, s 50 allows the consumer to use that information as forming a term of the contract.

Table 4.4 Remedies and implications

The right	Available remedy
Service to be performed with reasonable care and skill (**s 49**)	The right to require a repeat performance (**s 55**), and if that is impossible, or not done in a reasonable time or without significant inconvenience, the right to a price reduction (**s 56**)
Information about the trader or service to be binding (**s 50**)	The right to a reduction in price (**s 56**)
Service to be performed within a reasonable time (**s 52**)	The right to a reduction in price (**s 55**)

Reasonable price to be paid for a service (s 51)

This section applies to a contract to supply a service if the consumer has not paid a price for the service, the contract does not expressly identify/establish a price, or the contract is silent on how the price is to be reached. In such circumstances, s 51 holds that the contract is to be treated as including a term that the consumer must pay a reasonable price for the service, and no more. What is a reasonable price is a question of fact for the courts to determine in the specific circumstances.

Service to be performed within a reasonable time (s 52)

Where a contract to supply a service does not expressly fix the time for the service to be performed, it does not identify how it is to be fixed, and the information that is to be treated under s 50 as included in the contract does not fix the time either, the contract is to be treated as including a term that the trader must perform the service within a reasonable time. Reasonableness, as with s 51, is determined on the basis of a question of fact.

In the event that a trader seeks to exclude their liability for breach of guaranteed terms (ie those relating to the exercise of reasonable care and skill, or information about the trader or service which is considered to be a term of the contract), s 57 establishes that the exclusion will not be binding on the consumer. Further, the consumer will always possess the right to seek a refund of the price of the service where there has been a breach of the terms as identified earlier. Any term or clause inserted into a contract which seeks to restrict the trader's liability to an amount which is less than a contract price will not be binding or enforceable. Note also that where the restriction in liability in the contract relates to a price in excess of the contract price, such a clause may be accepted where it satisfies the test of fairness (s 62).

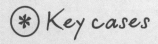

✱ Key cases

Case	Facts	Principle
Bartlett v Sidney Marcus Ltd [1965] 1 WLR 1013	Defects in a car were pointed out to the buyer before purchasing from a dealer. The claimant later sought damages on the basis of **SOGA 1979 s 14** when remedying the defect proved significantly more expensive than the discount offered by the dealer. The claim for damages failed.	Bartlett's claim was based on a breach of **s 14(1) and (2) SOGA 1979**, but the Court of Appeal held that there was no breach. Generally, quality of goods, even those purchased second-hand from a dealer, would allow protection but the defects had been brought to the buyer's attention before the sale.

Case	Facts	Principle
Rowland v Divall [1923] 2 KB 500	The defendant (unwittingly) purchased a stolen motorcar from a rogue and later resold it to the claimant dealer. When the identity of the vehicle was discovered, the dealer successfully claimed for the return of the money paid.	The requirement of good title is included in **SOGA 1979 s 12** and is an implied term into contracts for the sale of goods.
Smith v Eric S Bush [1990] 1 AC 831	The claimant purchased a house on the basis of the defendant's negligent valuation report but the contract provided for an exclusion clause disclaiming any liability for negligence in this report. Serious defects in the property led to substantial losses which the claimant attempted to recover.	The clause had been correctly incorporated into the contract but the House of Lords held the clause to be unreasonable under **UCTA 1977 s 2(2)**. It would be unfair and unreasonable to place potential risk of loss on a buyer for the negligence and incompetence of a surveyor providing a valuation.

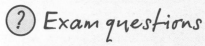 (?) Exam questions

Problem question

Sarah visits the local high street shop and purchases the following goods. With reference to statute and case law identify any legal consequences:

1. Sarah purchases a 'luxury, deep-filled duck-down pillow' to help her sleep. She uses the pillow and the following morning has suffered an allergic reaction and has a severe rash.

2. Sarah purchases a catapult for her son that breaks during the first use and injures her son's eye.

3. Sarah decides she requires a new pair of training shoes for the gym. She selects the pair described as having 'gel-filled soles' and being suitable for running on a treadmill. When Sarah uses the trainers, they begin to fall apart during the first gym session and she discovers the soles are not 'gel-filled' as advertised.

Advise Sarah on her rights.

An outline answer is included at the end of the book.

Exam questions

✳✳✳✳✳✳✳✳✳✳

Essay question

Critically assess the mechanisms utilized by the courts to differentiate terms as conditions and warranties and the effectiveness of the parties' attempts to define the terms in advance. What impact did the 'breach-based' approach have in adding certainty to the definition of terms?

 Online Resources

To see an outline answer to this question log on to www.oup.com/lawrevision/

#5

Contract IV: discharge of contract and remedies for breach

Key facts

- Contracts can be discharged in numerous ways—through performance, agreement, frustration, or breach.

- In the event of frustration, the parties can establish their own remedies or they can rely on the provisions developed through the **Law Reform (Frustrated Contracts) Act 1943**.

- Remedies have been established through the common law and equity.

- Damages are the primary remedy in most cases, but **equitable remedies** include specific performance, injunctions, and rectification.

- The innocent party must proactively (albeit reasonably) attempt to **mitigate** their losses following a breach of contract.

- The courts will usually identify the award of damages following a breach. However, the parties may agree such awards in advance (called liquidated damages) insofar as they are not a penalty clause.

Introduction

Remedies is an essential part of studying contract law as it frequently forms part of an examination question involving some wider aspect—offer and acceptance, conditions and warranties, etc. It may also be used to examine your understanding of the available remedies and the mechanisms used by the courts in quantifying the amount (award).

Revision tip

Ensure you are confident in determining how the courts assess the remedy of damages, but also when equitable remedies may be more appropriate. Identify how the courts expect the innocent party to behave in order to avail themselves of these remedies. Equitable remedies are powerful weapons in cases of breach and should be considered before you attempt an answer.

Under the normal rules of contract, a party is only discharged from a contract when they have completed the obligations under it (complete performance). Having completed the contract, each party is free of further obligations.

A failure to complete the contract may lead to a **breach of contract** claim, although situations exist where the parties may release each other from further obligations (discharge by agreement) or where the contract may have been partially or substantially performed (lacking complete performance). Further, the contract may have become radically different from that envisaged, or impossible to perform. In such instances, there is no breach as the contract has been **frustrated**. See Fig 5.1 for an overview of the forms of discharge of contract.

Figure 5.1 Discharge of contract

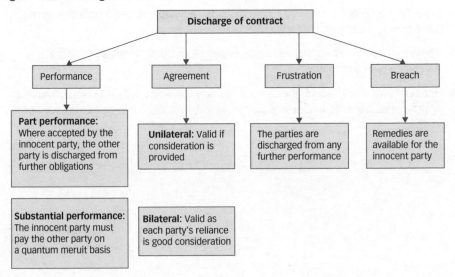

Discharge through performance

The most obvious form of discharge is through the parties' completion of their obligations and the contract being completely performed. However, a strict interpretation of this rule led to harsh consequences. *Cutter v Powell* [1795] involved an 'entire contract' whereby payment was made when the entire contract was completed. Here, the person died just before the completion of the contract and his widow was unable to recover any payment for the work he had completed (remedies now available through frustration did not exist at the time). A more fair system of divisible contracts, that is, broken down into smaller units, is now applied. Payment here is made in instalments rather than a single full amount on completion (*Ritchie v Atkinson* [1808]). Contracts of employment are examples of divisible contracts.

Part performance

There may exist situations where a contract is not fully completed, and the other party voluntarily accepts a partial performance (*Sumpter v Hedges* [1898]). Acceptance of the partial performance discharges the party from any further obligations under the contract and the innocent party must pay an appropriate proportion of the price (on the basis of a *quantum meruit* assessment).

Substantial performance

Where a substantial proportion of the contract has been completed, the innocent party has an obligation to pay, taking into account the shortcomings of the contract (*Hoeing v Isaacs* [1952]). Note: the obligation only exists where there has been 'substantial' performance (*Bolton v Mahadeva* [1972]).

A claim for a partial or substantial performance (on *quantum meruit*) of the contract may be made if the full and complete performance of the contract was prevented through the other party's actions (*Planche v Colburn* [1831]).

Discharge through agreement

The parties may agree between themselves that they no longer wish to continue with the contract, and therefore release each other from their obligations. As this is in effect a new contract, varying a contract requires the formalities as identified in Chapter 2 (specifically consideration to make the contract enforceable).

- Unilateral discharge: if one party has completed their part of the contract and the other party wishes to be released from their obligations which are outstanding, such an agreement will be allowed, but only legally binding, if consideration is provided.

- Bilateral discharge: if both parties have obligations outstanding under the contract, then if both agree to release each other from further obligations, the contract will be discharged by these mutual exchanges of promises. That both parties release each other will be good consideration and stop any legal rights under the contract.

Discharge through frustration

Frustration is a doctrine developed by the courts in order to offer relief in circumstances whereby a contract could not be performed or had become radically different from that contemplated, and this was neither of the parties' fault.

Frustration results, on the frustrating event, in the parties being discharged from any further performance in the contract and any money already paid is returned (at the discretion of the court).

There are several examples of what may amount to frustration and, whilst each case is decided on its own merits, there are common themes that aid in identifying what may be held to be frustration.

Examples of frustrating events:

- the subject matter of the contract ceases to exist (*Taylor v Caldwell* [1863]);
- a person engaged under a contract of personal service becomes permanently unavailable (*Condor v The Barron Knights* [1966]);
- an event central to the contract has not occurred (*Krell v Henry* [1903]);
- the contract cannot be performed in the manner specified (*Nickoll & Knight v Ashton, Edridge & Co* [1901]);
- the contract becomes illegal to perform following the contract being established (*Fibrosa Spolka Akcyjna v Fairbairn Lawson Combe Barbour* [1943]);
- the contract becomes radically different from that envisaged (*Davis Contractors Ltd v Fareham Urban DC* [1956]).

Limits to frustration

If one of the parties has deliberately or negligently led to the contract failing, they must accept the loss and/or compensate the innocent party (*The Super Servant II (sub nom Lauritzen v Wijsmuller)* [1990]).

Effects of frustration

When the court has determined that a contract has been frustrated, the contract ends as soon as the frustrating event occurs.

As frustration typically affects businesses more than consumer contracts, the courts have encouraged the parties to make provisions for such events in the contract. In the absence of contractual provisions, assistance has been provided through the **Law Reform (Frustrated Contracts) Act 1943**.

The statute provides:

- that all money still owing under the contract ceases to be due;
- all money paid is recoverable (at the court's discretion);

- the money returned includes deposits (pre-payments) and expenses that, before the case law and statutory interventions, resulted in such losses 'lying where they fell'.

The harshness of the application of losses 'lying where they fell' in this respect can be seen in *Appleby v Myers* (1867) where a contractor's expenses for labour and materials lost following a fire were not recoverable as the contract stipulated payment on completion. Section 1(2) of the statute would enable the return of expenses.
And

- any valuable benefit gained has to be compensated for. This assessment of a valuable benefit gained is somewhat difficult in that the legislation does not provide a definition— see *BP Exploration Co (Libya) Ltd v Hunt (No 2)* [1982].

The provisions listed earlier do not apply if the parties make their own provisions for the effect of frustration (s 2(3)).

Force majeure clauses

To restrict the possibility of a frustrating event ending the contract, the parties may draft a *force majeure* **clause**. This clause involves two elements:

- some level of foreseeability as to the possible frustrating event; and
- that the event was in the contemplation of the parties at the time of contracting.

Examples may include provisions for bad weather, difficulties in supplies of labour, and so on. Such clauses are valid and will be accepted by the courts if it is the true intention of the parties and the clause is not designed to limit the exposure of one of the parties to liability for breach.

Discharge through breach

As identified in Chapter 4, in the event of a breach of a term of a contract, that term will be identified as a condition or warranty.

- A breach of a condition gives the injured party the option both to terminate (**repudiate**) the contract and to claim damages. In some instances it may be advantageous for the injured party to claim damages but also to continue with (known as 'affirming') the contract.
- In the case of a warranty, this being a lesser term, the injured party is entitled to damages, but they must still continue with the obligations under the contract.

In the event that the full contractual obligations owed by one of the parties are not fulfilled, or the performance is substantially less than could be expected, the innocent party may treat this as a complete breach of the contract.

MSC Mediterranean Shipping Company S.A. v Cottonex Anstalt [2016] EWCA Civ 789

The case involved the repudiation of a contract. The question for the Court of Appeal was whether it was possible to affirm a contract where the party in breach had no means possible to perform the contract. The Court held that in the event of a repudiatory breach, the innocent party is not able to affirm the contract if further performance of it is not possible. This would be the case where the breach has the effect of frustrating the commercial purpose of the contract. The judgment also included *obiter* comments which are interesting for the assessment of the consequences of breach of contract. An innocent party will not be able to affirm a contract if the purpose of this action is simply to allow it to continue to claim damages (the innocent party would not have a 'legitimate interest' in maintaining the contract).

Anticipatory breach

Situations may arise where one of the parties recognizes (or is informed) that the other party is not going to fulfil their contractual obligations. This is referred to as an anticipatory breach. If accepted, anticipatory breach enables the claimant to treat the contract as repudiated and seek damages before the date of the agreed performance of the contract (*Hochester v De La Tour* [1853]).

Alternatively, the innocent party can choose to wait for the time when performance was due, and when the contract is breached through incomplete performance, seek a remedy (actual breach). There is no obligation on the innocent party to accept the anticipatory breach, but as soon as they do, reasonable steps must be taken to **mitigate** losses (*Clea Shipping Corporation v Bulk Oil International* [1984]). The damages available for breach and anticipatory breach are the same (see the following section).

In *The Golden Victory (Golden Strait Corporation v Nippon Yusen Kubishka Kaisha)* [2007]), the House of Lords considered that where a charterer of a ship wrongfully repudiated a charterparty, and the innocent party accepted the repudiation, the damages awarded could be restricted. The contract contained a clause that the charterers would be allowed to cancel the contract in the event of war with Iraq (which was a possibility when the contract was formed). It was further known to both parties that this option would have been exercised had war broken out. The contract was repudiated before the outbreak of war, but the war was effective before the term of the contract was completed. As such, the Lords held that with this knowledge, as opposed to only assessing damages at the time of the breach, a more accurate assessment could be achieved along the lines of 'fair compensation'. Hence, the assessment of damages was altered from the 'traditional' approach.

Remedies for breach

In the event that a contract is not performed, or obligations under the contract are not fulfilled, the innocent party may be entitled to compensation.

Under the common law, this is usually in the form of damages (a money payment), but may also involve equitable remedies such as **specific performance**, **injunctions**, and **rectification**.

Damages

Any breach of contract entitles the injured party to damages, irrespective of whether the term is classified as a 'condition' or 'warranty'.

Damages exist to compensate the injured party for any losses sustained under the breach of the contract. The purpose of damages is not to punish the transgressor, or put the injured party in a better financial position than they would have achieved through the completion of the contract.

Damages can be either:

- **liquidated**: the parties have anticipated the consequences of the breach, determined the level of damages to be paid, and included this in the contract; or
- **unliquidated**: determined by the court having heard the arguments/evidence (more frequently used).

In order for the courts to assess damages, to ensure fairness, there are underlying principles that must be adhered to. These are:

- the damages must not be too remote;
- they must be quantifiable by the court;
- they must be recognized as damages in English law; and
- the injured party must have sought to mitigate their losses as far as is reasonable.

Remoteness of damage

The party in breach will not be liable for damages that are deemed too remote—although see *The Golden Victory (Golden Strait Corporation v Nippon Yusen Kubishka Kaisha)* [2007] regarding fair compensation.

✅ Looking for extra marks?

If you are asked to consider the award (and calculation) of damages, especially in relation to cases of anticipatory breach, remember the decision in *The Golden Victory*. Assess whether it will change the tactics of the injured party, particularly in terms of anticipatory breach. Will the injured party seek to claim damages immediately, and will the defendant attempt to halt proceedings to see if it can benefit from a delay? Does this have any implications for dispute resolution generally?

The general rules for assessing the remoteness of damage include the following considerations established in *Hadley v Baxendale* (1854):

- do the damages arise naturally in the normal and ordinary course of the contract; and
- are the damages within the 'reasonable contemplation' of the parties?

The legal reasoning in *Hadley v Baxendale* was continued in *Victoria Laundry v Newman Industries* [1949], where a delay in delivering an industrial boiler for commercial launderers would allow damages to be claimed for the subsequent associated lost profits (the first point listed), but this did not extend to possible lucrative contracts that could have been won had the boiler been delivered as expected (the second point).

Having established that the damages claimed were reasonable in the circumstances of the case, the next issue for the courts is how to quantify the losses.

Quantum

The methods a court may use to assess the measure of damage are:

- **reliance damages**: designed to prevent the injured party from suffering financial harm and placing them in the position in which they were before the contract had been established;
- **expectation damages**: identifies what the injured party would have achieved from the successful completion of the contract, and seeks to place them, as far as money can, in that position.

In assessing the quantum of damages the courts will consider:

- any loss of a bargain/opportunity the injured party has suffered;
- whether the parties have identified any 'agreed' damages in advance in the contract; and
- the injured party's duty to mitigate their losses.

In the event of breach, damages is a remedy designed to award the cost of rectifying the loss, and provide compensation for any other foreseeable, consequential losses.

The Supreme Court in *Morris-Garner v One Step (Support) Ltd* [2018] reaffirmed the compensatory nature of damages and that the claimant has the duty to quantify the losses incurred. This should be performed as accurately and reliably as possible (even where specific evidence may be lacking). It further reminded lower courts that damages payments (at common law) are claimed as of right and their award is on the basis of legal principle. The claimant is not permitted to elect how those damages are to be assessed.

Damages are limited to where the courts see the award as being reasonable. The following case, it can be argued, demonstrates where the courts do not provide 'adequate' damages following a breach.

Ruxley Electronics and Construction Ltd v Forsyth [1995] 3 WLR 118

Ruxley was engaged to build a swimming pool, being 7 feet, 6 inches at its deepest end. Upon completion, the depth of the swimming pool was only 6 feet. It was estimated that it would cost £21,560 for the pool to be rebuilt to the required depth but following this breach of contract, Forsyth was only awarded £2,500 for loss of amenity, not the cost of rebuilding. Cost of rebuilding was considered by the House of Lords as 'unfair enrichment' and unreasonable in the circumstances.

Damages for injured feelings/loss of enjoyment

Traditionally, in determining the level of damages applicable in a case, injured feelings or loss of enjoyment suffered have been ignored (*Addis v Gramophone* [1909]). This is often because of the problems inherent in quantifying such damages and the potential of opening the floodgates for claimants. However, where the whole basis of the contract is, for example, for enjoyment, such damages are recoverable (*Jarvis v Swans Tours* [1972]—involving a holiday).

Mitigation of loss

The injured party has an obligation to limit the losses which they incur as a result of the breach of contract. However, the duty is not absolute and an element of reasonableness is introduced whereby the injured party does not have to take unnecessary steps to reduce loss (*Brace v Calder* [1895]).

Agreed/liquidated damages

Businesses may attempt to estimate the damages to be paid in the event of a breach at the agreement stage of the formation of a contract. These are known as agreed or liquidated damages.

For liquidated damages to be accepted, it must be a genuine pre-estimate of the loss rather than a **penalty clause**. A penalty clause is a threat against breaching the contract and will not be enforceable.

There are tests that may help to distinguish liquidated damages from a penalty clause. In *Dunlop Pneumatic Tyre Co v New Garage and Motor Co* [1915] the court held that the following factors should be considered:

- The use of the words 'penalty' or 'liquidated damages' may illustrate the nature of the clause but this is not conclusive.

- The essence of liquidated damages is a genuine pre-estimate of damage.

- The question whether a sum stipulated is a penalty or liquidated damages is a question to be decided on the terms and circumstances of each contract, and judged at the time of the making of the contract, not as at the time of the breach.

- It will be held to be a penalty if the sum stipulated for is extravagant and unconscionable in amount compared with the greatest loss that could conceivably be proved to have followed from the breach.
- There is a presumption (but no more) that it is a penalty when 'a single lump sum' is made payable by way of compensation, on the occurrence of one or more or all of several events, some of which may occasion serious, and others trifling, damage.

Revision tip

The courts will not rigidly follow these tests as they are merely a guide, but they do provide a useful reference to follow in what may prove to be a complex enquiry.

Recently, the Supreme Court revisited the issue of penalty clauses in *Cavendish Square Holding BV v Talal El Makdessi and ParkingEye Limited v Beavis* [2015] (joined cases). *Cavendish* involved an agreement between the parties where Makdessi would sell to Cavendish a controlling stake in his company. Importantly, if Makdessi breached certain restrictive covenants, he would not be entitled to agreed payments of $44 million and Cavendish would be entitled to exercise an option to purchase remaining shares at a reduced value. Upon a breach by Makdessi and Cavendish's attempt to enforce the relevant clauses, the argument as to whether this amounted to a penalty clause was raised. Ultimately, the Supreme Court upheld the traditional test for penalty clauses, although it commented that such clauses should not be assessed on whether or not it is intended to be a detriment, rather the test should be on whether the innocent party had a 'legitimate interest to protect'. This should lead to much greater care being taken in the drafting of (commercial) contracts, where clauses containing a 'genuine pre-estimate of loss' actually outline what the legitimate business interest being protected is (and hence the clause is more likely to be accepted rather than being successfully challenged as a penalty clause). This is likely to have significant effects in the construction industry where such clauses are commonplace.

When considering the legality of a clause pre-empting the award of damages, remember the judgment provided: '[T]he modern cases thus appear to accept that a clause providing for payment on a breach of a sum of money that exceeds the amount that a court would award as compensation . . . may not be regarded as penal if it can be justified commercially and if its predominant purpose is not to deter breach.' This gives the party attempting to rely on such a clause significant latitude. As a rule of thumb, insofar as such a charge is not extravagant and unconscionable, it will be allowed as a pre-estimate of loss.

Equitable remedies

The courts will generally provide damages as a remedy for breach of contract wherever possible (as this is usually the simplest form of a remedy).

Situations exist where money would not provide an appropriate remedy, or would be unjust due to the nature of the contract which has been breached. This led to the development of the equitable remedies. Being 'equitable' remedies, they are awarded at the courts' discretion.

Specific performance

Specific performance is a remedy most frequently used in the sale of unique items—land, antiques, etc. It is a court order compelling the party in breach to perform their contractual obligations. As an equitable remedy, it must also be available (potentially) to both parties and where it would not cause unreasonable hardship (*Co-operative Insurance Society v Argyll Stores* [1997]).

Specific performance cannot be ordered in the following types of contract:

- Contracts for personal services; or
- Contracts requiring constant supervision by the courts.

In *Rainbow Estates v Tokenhold* [1998], specific performance was granted compelling a tenant to carry out repairs to the landlord's premises (as identified in the contract) as once the repairs were completed, no further supervision would be necessary.

Revision tip

The issue to remember is of 'constant' supervision that would limit the remedy's application.

Injunctions

There are two main types of injunction available to the courts—mandatory injunctions and prohibitory injunctions (although interim injunctions may be granted prior to a full hearing to prevent injury to the claimant):

- mandatory injunctions compel the party to perform the contract;
- prohibitory injunctions (more common) stop a party from breaching the contract.

Failing to follow the order of an injunction will result in the transgressor being guilty of contempt of court—a potentially very serious offence.

As with specific performance, injunctions will only be used where damages would be inadequate and the issuing of the injunction must be reasonable.

Rectification

The remedy of rectification enables a written document (eg a contract) to be changed (eg including/removing clauses) more accurately to reflect the terms that were identified in the oral agreement subsequently placed in writing (*A Roberts & Co v Leicestershire CC* [1961]).

In order for a claim for rectification to succeed:

- the parties must have established an oral contract that identified the terms of the agreement;
- these terms did not change from the oral agreement until it was written; and
- the written contract does not accurately provide what was stated in the oral agreement.

Key cases

****

> ### Revision tip
> The remedy allows the written document to be altered accurately to reflect the parties' oral agreement, but importantly not simply to alter it to what one of the parties wanted to have included.

Rectification may also be available where one of the parties believes that the contract reflects the intentions of the parties, but it does not, and the other party is aware of this mistake (*Commission for the New Towns v Cooper (GB) Ltd* **[1995]**).

Time limit to a claim

The **Limitation Act 1980 s 5** provides that a breach of a simple contract claim must be made within six years from when the right to the action arose. In the case of contracts made under deed, the claim must be established within 12 years (**s 8(1)**).

There is no statutory provision for time limits to claim under the equitable remedies but, as these are equitable, they must be sought within a reasonable time.

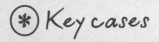 Key cases

Case	Facts	Principle
Hadley v Baxendale (1854) 156 ER 145	Hadley sent its only mill crankshaft to be delivered by Baxendale to a third party for repair. Baxendale unnecessarily delayed the delivery and caused Hadley lost profits. Baxendale's defence was that it did not know Hadley had sent its only crankshaft the delay of which would result in a total stoppage in production.	In the event of a breach, damages should be based on what may fairly and reasonably be considered arising naturally; and it should have been in the contemplation of both parties at the time they established the contract.
Ocean Trawlers v Maritime National Fish [1935] UKPC 1	Maritime National Fish entered into a contract for the hire of a fishing trawler on the basis that it would be granted the necessary licences for this vessel and the others it already owned. When fewer licences were granted than required, it claimed the contract of hire was frustrated.	The case demonstrated the limit to frustration. The claimant was at fault for entering into the contract before ensuring the required licences were issued. The contract was neither radically different from that contracted for nor impossible to perform.

Case	Facts	Principle
Ruxley Electronics and Construction Ltd v Forsyth [1995] 3 WLR 118	The parties contracted for the construction of a swimming pool but it was built at smaller depth than agreed. Damages were awarded for loss of amenity and not for the cost of rebuilding (which would have put the innocent party in the position in which he would have been had the breach not occurred).	Loss of amenity was considered a fairer assessment of damages as the cost of rebuilding would have been an unjust enrichment and unreasonable.
Taylor v Caldwell [1863] 3 B & S 826	A music hall was hired for various performances but was destroyed by fire before the events could be held.	This case established frustration of the contract. The event preventing performance of the contract was neither party's fault.

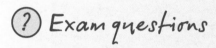 Exam questions

Problem question

Junichiro books a holiday with Super Skiing Holidays Plc which specializes in holidays for single people. Junichiro books for a two-week holiday to a resort in Switzerland. The brochure describes the resort as hosting a 'house party' where live entertainment will be provided every night and there will be several people with whom to meet and enjoy the resort.

When Junichiro arrives he is unhappy with the quality of the room and the food is of a very poor standard. The only ski boots available are too small for his feet and the skis were designed for children—there were no adult sizes. The entertainment consists of a local plumber who provides his Elvis Presley impersonation for 30 minutes each night on his way home from work. Junichiro is joined at the resort by three other guests, all of whom are French and do not speak English, and they leave after five days—leaving Junichiro the only person at the resort for the remainder of the holiday.

When Junichiro returns home he complains to Super Skiing Holidays but they state it was not their problem and he cannot claim damages for the loss of enjoyment of his vacation.

Advise Junichiro.

An outline answer is included at the end of the book.

Exam questions

✴✴✴✴✴✴✴✴✴✴

Essay question

With reference to case law, identify the principles underlying the courts' assessment of damages. In particular, critically assess the application of remoteness of damage and how it controls the award of expectation losses.

 Online Resources

To see an outline answer to this question log on to www.oup.com/lawrevision/

#6
Law of torts

Key facts

- It is important to recognize the differences between contractual and tortious liability. Contractual liability involves a voluntary undertaking of obligations whilst tortious liability involves obligations that may be imposed by law.

- A party must take reasonable care not to negligently cause harm.

- Negligence involves a breach of a duty to take care, owed in law by the defendant to the claimant, causing the claimant damage/loss.

- Not all claimants have to demonstrate loss/damage. Claims under trespass, for example, will often involve the award of nominal damages where no 'harm' has been sustained.

- Common defences to torts are illegality, consent, contributory negligence, and necessity.

- Private nuisance involves unlawful interference with another person's enjoyment of their land/property which causes the claimant loss (and the loss/damage was reasonably foreseeable).

- When products cause injury/loss, rather than attempting to claim negligence, a claimant may seek protection through the **Consumer Protection Act (CPA) 1987**.

Introduction

'Tort' derives from the French word for 'wrong' and is essentially a civil wrong that entitles the injured party to the remedy of compensation (damages). This remedy has the aim of placing the victim back into the position in which they were (as far as money can) before the tort was committed. A significant tort is negligence and as such it frequently appears in assessments. Other torts that must be understood include **nuisance** (both public and private forms), the statutory protection of the **CPA 1987** and the **Occupiers' Liability Acts**, and the doctrine of **vicarious liability**.

Fault liability

The law imposes a duty to take reasonable care to not negligently or intentionally cause damage. Claims of negligence involve fault liability; someone is at fault and this enables the injured party to seek compensation for the resultant loss/injury.

Some forms of tortious liability may also be imposed in the absence of fault. For example, the doctrine of vicarious liability results in one person being held liable for the torts of another (eg an employer liable for the torts of their employees; a principal liable for the torts of their agent). Further, fault is removed in claims under the **CPA 1987** where the liability is (at least in theory) strict.

Time limits

The **Limitation Act 1980 s 2**, provides that actions in tort must be brought within six years of the date of the event giving rise to the right of action. Claims for personal injury, however, must be brought within three years of either the date on which the tort was committed or from when the injury attributable to the **tortfeasor** (the person who committed the tort) became known (**s 11**). These time limits differ where the claimant is suffering a mental disorder or is a minor.

Difference between tortious and contractual liability

- Contractual liability imposes obligations only when these are entered into voluntarily.
- Tortious liability may be imposed on persons and organizations (sometimes) without their knowledge or the awareness of the potential extent of this liability.

Remember that there may be several legal claims/issues involving the same scenario—for example, a scenario may involve a criminal action *and* a tort claim (eg an employee in a factory being injured through the use of dangerous and faulty equipment). Where the claimant has suffered a loss and injury, it is for the claimant to elect to pursue each element of their claim.

Negligence

Negligence is the breach of a duty to take care, owed in law by the defendant to the claimant, causing the claimant damage (see Fig 6.1).

Figure 6.1 Stages for a negligence claim

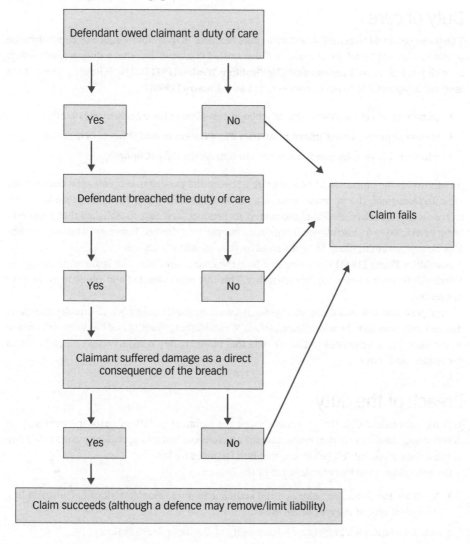

Negligence

****

In order to establish a successful claim in negligence, (all) three tests must be satisfied. Each of these will be discussed in turn:

1. the defendant owes the claimant a duty of care;
2. there was a breach of that duty;
3. there has been consequential damage as a result of the breach (and the damage is actionable).

Duty of care

The three sub-tests to establish a duty to take reasonable care not to injure or cause damage to others may not be necessary where it is a settled matter of law that a duty is owed—such as with road users and pedestrians (*Nettleship v Weston* [1971]). The following three-stage test will be applicable to novel claims (such as in *Caparo* [1990]):

- **proximity** of relationship—the 'neighbour' test (*Donoghue v Stevenson* [1932]);
- foreseeability of loss (*Caparo Industries Plc v Dickman and Others* [1990]); and
- whether it is fair, just, and reasonable to impose the duty (*Caparo*).

'Proximity' is the closeness of relationship between the parties that creates the duty to take care. In *Donoghue*, the manufacturer of a product was held liable for damage sustained by anyone who could have used, and consumed, its product. The case established that proximity is not restricted to a close physical proximity but can be extended to anyone who may reasonably be seen as being likely to be affected by the defendant's actions.

Bourhill v Young [1943] demonstrated how the courts deal with the issue of proximity of relationship and the link with foreseeability. This test was extended and added to in the case of *Caparo*.

'Fair, just, and reasonable' is an argument based on public policy which enables the court discretion to consider the wider implications of establishing liability and has been referred to as the 'floodgates' argument (although note that public policy considerations extend beyond floodgates concerns).

Breach of the duty

Having established that the defendant owed the claimant a duty of care, the next step in determining liability is to determine that they have breached this duty. This means establishing that the defendant fell below the standard required by law.

Breach is identified by consideration of the factors:

- Whether the defendant exposed the claimant to unreasonable risk of harm (including foreseeability of the risk of harm).
- What was the social utility and desirability of the defendant's action(s).

- The cost and practicality of the measures needed to minimize the risk (*compare Bolton v Stone* [1951] and *Miller v Jackson* [1977]).

- Whether the defendant breached the 'reasonable man' standard—*Blyth v Birmingham Waterworks Co* [1856].

Revision Tip

The defendant must take into account the shortcomings of others, and there is an obligation imposed on defendants to display appropriate levels of skill—such as compliance with professional standards (*Bolam v Friern Hospital Management Committee* [1957]).

Consequential damage

Having established that a duty of care is owed, which the defendant has breached, for a negligence claim to be successful a causal link between the breach and the loss/damage suffered by the claimant must be demonstrated. This link (or chain of events) may be broken by a new act (a *novus actus interveniens*). If a new act, independent of the defendant's action, occurs and is sufficiently independent, it may stop the imposition of liability on the (first) defendant.

This loss/damage must be a type recognized by the law.

Causation in fact

The court will examine the facts of the case and ascertain whether the defendant had caused or contributed to the claimant's injury or suffering.

If the damage would not have happened *but for* a particular fault then that fault is the cause of the damage – if it would have happened just the same, fault or not fault, the fault is not the cause of damage (*Barnett v Chelsea and Kensington Hospital Management Committee* [1969]).

Causation in law

The defendant is not liable for every consequence of their wrong. If there is some intervening act that causes the damage to the claimant then the (first) defendant will not be held responsible in negligence. If the damage sustained was too remote, then it would be unreasonable to hold the defendant responsible.

Remoteness of damage involves the test of reasonable foreseeability. If the reasonable man/person could not foresee the consequences of the action, in terms of the type of harm occurring, then the claim will be defeated (*The Wagon Mound* [1961]).

Revision Tip

It is not necessary that the extent of the loss is foreseeable but rather it is the type of loss that must be foreseeable.

Attempts to mitigate losses will not, in most cases, result in the chain of causation being broken (*Corr v IBC Vehicles Ltd* [2008]).

Defences

Consent

Consent (*volenti non fit injuria*—no actionable injury is done to a consenting party) is a complete defence and is available where there has been an express agreement to the particular risk of damage. It may also (exceptionally) be implied from the conduct of the claimant due to the actions of volunteering (eg acting as a rescuer) or by accepting entering into a situation involving risk (*Morris v Murray* [1990]).

The defence of consent is not available simply because a party (eg an employee) is aware of the risk of injury at the workplace, and continues to carry out their duties (*Smith v Baker & Sons* [1891]). The courts will require an outward sign of consent in relation to the inherent risk.

Volenti may be a defence in employment situations where a deliberate act has been undertaken against the express orders of the employer.

ICI v Shatwell [1964] 3 WLR 329

The claimant and a colleague, qualified shot-firers, made a test of an electrical circuit for firing explosives without taking the appropriate cover. They were injured, but *volenti* enabled the employer to present a complete defence on (both) actions of vicarious liability and **breach of a statutory duty**. The claimants had agreed to take this action knowing the danger and the action was contrary to the employer's instructions and statutory regulations.

Contributory negligence

Contributory negligence is a partial defence. The claimant is referred to as having 'contributed to their own misfortune' and if they have been at fault in any activities that have led to their injury, the court will reflect this in the damages awarded (**Law Reform (Contributory Negligence) Act 1945 s 1(1)**). The Court of Appeal has also held that the claimant may even be entitled to succeed in an action for damages where they are 60 per cent liable for their injuries (*Green v Bannister* [2003]).

Jackson v Murray & another [2015] UKSC 5

The Supreme Court heard a case involving a 13-year old victim of a speeding motorist. At first instance the court found the victim to be 90 per cent responsible for her injuries. On appeal, this contribution was reduced to 70 per cent and the Supreme Court further reduced her contribution to 50 per cent. The significance of the case lies in the different views on the facts of the case by the appeal courts. Generally, appeal courts do not interfere with the court at first instance's assessment of the facts. However, here the appeal courts, on two occasions, reduced the victim's contribution to the damage sustained. In the future, parties may be inclined to appeal decisions and gamble on the prospect of an appeal court challenging the factual decision-making of the court at first instance.

Necessity

A defence to trespass actions is available where the tortfeasor acted in a way so as to prevent a greater harm occurring. To be successful, the defendant must demonstrate:

- there was imminent danger to a person or to property; and
- the actions taken were reasonable in the circumstances.

These are subjective tests that will be assessed by the court (see *Esso Petroleum Co Ltd v Southport Corporation* [1956]).

Illegality

Illegality is included here to demonstrate the limits to claims for negligence. Instances exist where a claimant has committed an illegal act and as such they are prevented from raising a negligence action (*Ashton v Turner* [1980]).

Remedies

Damages

The aim of damages is to place the injured party, as far as money can, in the position in which they were before the tort was committed (ie, it is compensatory).

Damages for personal injury suffered may incorporate any direct losses (eg loss of earnings, medical expenses, etc). Further losses that may be compensable include damages for pain and suffering, loss of amenity, and so on.

The damages awarded in relation to property are to compensate the claimant for loss, and this will involve cost of restoration and may involve an element of compensation where a replacement of the goods/property was difficult to achieve. Awards of damages are subject to a requirement for the injured party to mitigate their losses.

The Court of Appeal, in *M Wellesley Partners LLP v Withers LLP* [2015] determined that in the event where concurrent causes of action (claims for loss) exist in both tort and contract, the courts will assess the issue of recoverability of loss according to the principle used in the contractual test. This means that unlike in tort where the court will use the test of 'reasonable foreseeability' when determining remoteness, here the test will be whether the damages claimable were within the contemplation of the parties. The contractual test is more restrictive than that used in tort as there are times where loss may be reasonably foreseeable, yet still not be within the reasonable contemplation of the parties.

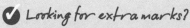 **Looking for extra marks?**

If you have a question which involves a potential for claims under contract and tort,—ie the claimant has a choice of defendants/issues—previous cases provide such an example: the liability of an engineer (see *Pirelli v Oscar Faber & Partners* [1983]) or a solicitor (see *Midland Bank v Hett Stubbs & Kemp* [1979]), consider carefully the prospect of choosing a torts action, where, assuming the other factors are equal, the remoteness test is broader and hence more favourable to the claimant.

Eggshell skull rule

There is an obligation to 'take your victim as you find them'—the 'eggshell skull' rule. Further, this concept has been applied to cases of psychiatric injuries. Lane J in *Malcolm v Broadhurst* [1970] described it as the 'eggshell personality'.

Nuisance

When a person unlawfully interferes with another's land, or the quiet enjoyment of the land, then the innocent party may have a claim under the tort of nuisance (private nuisance). In order to bring a successful claim of nuisance, the following features must be present:

- The interference affects the enjoyment of land/premises and this action may be brought by a person with a proprietary interest in it, a tenant, or a person with exclusive possession of land but with no title to it.

- There must be an element of damage associated with the nuisance (damage to the land and/or the claimant losing their enjoyment of the premises).

> ✔️ **Looking for extra marks?**
>
> The law has to balance competing interests—the right for the owner/occupier of land to quiet enjoyment of the property, and the business that has to make some noise/disruption in the processing of its product. It does so through assessment as to the unreasonableness of the defendant's use of the land:
>
> - The motives of the defendant are a relevant consideration—where the defendant has deliberately acted to cause a disturbance, the court will be more likely to hold this action as a nuisance (*Christie v Davey* [1893]).
> - The defendant will not be liable unless the damage suffered was of a type that was reasonably foreseeable by the defendant (*Cambridge Water Co v Eastern Counties Leather* [1994]).
> - Unusually sensitive (hypersensitive) claimants will not generally succeed in an action for nuisance where another person would not have been adversely affected.

Defences to nuisance claims

Statutory authority

Where a statute authorizes an act that is then subject to a claim of nuisance, the courts will assess whether the claim of nuisance is able to proceed (see *Allen v Gulf Oil Refining Ltd* [1981]).

Consent

If a party consents to a nuisance, then they are unlikely to succeed in an action. This is a complete defence and will apply where the defendant can establish that the injured party had accepted the danger of the noise, smell, vibration, or other nuisance, having been aware of its existence.

Revision tip

This is a grey area, as merely occupying land in the knowledge of a nuisance will not establish an effective defence of consent. It is the willingness to accept the possibility of the nuisance that is the key element. See *Leakey v National Trust* [1980].

Prescription

Here, a defence is available where the nuisance has been committed for over 20 years without complaint. It is important that the nuisance has been committed for 20 years, rather than simply the business that would have caused the nuisance having been carrying out that activity for that period of time.

Remedies

Damages

Damages are assessed in the same way as outlined earlier for negligence, and the duty of mitigation remains.

Injunction

Injunctions may be awarded at the discretion of the court and will involve a court order requiring the subject to stop committing the tort.

Abatement

This is an (exceptional) remedy enabling the injured party to take action to stop the nuisance. It is allowed where to initiate a legal action may be inappropriate or where immediate action is required.

Public nuisance

A public nuisance is a tort and a crime and involves acts or omissions that endanger the health or property of the public, or prevents the public from exercising rights to which they are entitled. The claimant must demonstrate that the nuisance has caused them greater damage than experienced by the public generally.

The defences of statutory authority, consent, and contributory negligence as outlined earlier are applicable to public nuisance, as are the remedies of injunction and damages. A further defence of act of God is also available (where applicable) in instances of public nuisance.

Pure economic loss

Where the claimant has 'only' suffered economic loss (as opposed to situations where it is linked to physical damage, for example loss of income following a car accident) the recovery, in damages, of such losses is very limited.

Pure economic loss

✳✳✳✳✳✳✳✳✳✳✳✳

Weller v Foot and Mouth Research Institute [1966] 1 QB 569

The defendants negligently allowed the foot and mouth virus to escape from their research laboratory with the consequence that cattle were destroyed and restrictions were imposed on the transport and trade of cattle in the affected area. The claimant was an auctioneer who had lost profits in sales due to the restrictions, and brought an action to recover the losses due to this negligent act. It was held that as this was a case of **pure economic loss**, the claim must fail.

Revision tip

It is important to note the limitation of success of claims when pure economic loss is suffered. In *Weller*, if the auctioneer was successful in claiming damages then could others so affected by the negligent act—suppliers of beef, consumers unable to purchase beef locally, and so on?

The general rule preventing claims based on pure economic loss is subject to exceptions—particularly in situations where a special relationship exists between the parties that elevate the defendant's responsibility to the claimant. For example, in *Ross v Caunters* [1980], a special relationship was established between a firm of solicitors and their client as it was reasonably foreseeable that a beneficiary could be affected by their negligence. However, in *Commissioners of Customs and Excise v Barclays Bank Plc* [2006] it was held that liability for pure economic loss will only be recoverable where:

- the person has a responsibility, or has assumed a responsibility, for their statement to the claimant and the claimant relies on that assumption of responsibility;
- the tests as established in *Caparo* [1990] are satisfied;
- a breach of duty can be established; and
- causation can be established.

An interesting case was heard by the Court of Appeal in relation to a professional offering advice in their area of expertise.

Lejonvarn v Burgess & Anor [2017] EWCA Civ 254

The case revisited the issue of the potential liability in negligence of a professional who offers 'advice' for free which causes the other party loss. An architect offered friends some advice on the landscaping of the garden in their £5 million home in London. When the project went wrong, the friends claimed £260,000 in damages from the architect. At the Court of Appeal, it was held that the architect was a professional offering a service and thus owed her friends a legal duty of care. It was however later accepted by Bowdery J that as the advice had been given in a non-commercial, informal, and social context, the architect could not be held responsible in damages in these circumstances.

Negligent misstatements

In some cases, businesses provide expert advice that clients and others rely on when investing money, making decisions, and so on, and when these involve statements negligently made, the recipient may suffer loss. This involves pure economic loss, but provides an avenue for redress where a special relationship between the parties has been demonstrated (*Hedley Byrne & Co v Heller* [1963]). *Hedley Byrne* also extends to the negligent provision of services (*Henderson v Merrett Syndicates Ltd* [1995]).

Negligent misstatements may enable a damages action where the following criteria are present:

- there must have been negligence when the statement was made;
- the statement must be given by an expert acting in the course of their expertise following a request by the claimant (or they had a right to receive the advice);
- there must be a duty of care owed to the person who acts on the statement—an assumption of responsibility;
- there must be reliance on the statement by the person(s) to whom it was addressed;
- there must be foreseeable loss arising out of the reliance;
- following *Caparo* [1990], it must be fair, just, and equitable to impose the duty.

Revision tip

Note that the exclusion clause in **Hedley Byrne** was allowed but, if used today, would have to satisfy the requirements of the **Unfair Contract Terms Act (UCTA) 1977** as being reasonable (consider **Smith v Eric S Bush** [1989]). UCTA 1977 only applies in business-to-business contracts, although similar protection is offered in business-to-consumer contracts under the **Consumer Rights Act (CRA) 2015**—see Chapter 4).

✔ Looking for extra marks?

Many cases have set out tests for the assessment of negligent misstatements—**Hedley Byrne & Co v Heller**, **James McNaughten v Hicks**, and **Yorkshire Enterprise Ltd v Robson Rhodes**. The House of Lords stated in **Commissioners for Customs and Excise v Barclays Bank Plc** that the tests outlined in these cases were correct, but they are fact-specific (specific to the cases to which they relate). Sweeping statements regarding the application of tests are not possible and cases must be considered on their facts. Bear this in mind if you face a question on this topic.

Vicarious liability

Employers may be held liable for the torts committed by their employees (and exceptionally by independent contractors) in the course of employment—'the servant must be engaged on his master's business and not off on a frolic of his own' (*Joel v Morison* [1834]).

Two tests are required to establish vicarious liability—1) the employee status of the tort-feasor and 2) that the tort was committed in their 'course of employment'. Tests to establish employment status are considered in Chapter 7 but when applied to vicarious liability, the case of *Cox v Ministry of Justice* [2014] is particularly important. Here the Court of Appeal held in a situation where the claimant was a catering manager at a prison, injured when an inmate working in the kitchen dropped a sack of food on her, that a claim for damages may be presented against the Ministry of Justice as the employer. The accident was caused by the negligence of a prisoner, but the court agreed that the law of vicarious liability had moved beyond the confines of liability only being attributable to a person engaged under a contract of service (an employee). In the present case the prisoner was, generally speaking, under the control of the employer (akin to an employment relationship), the work was done on behalf and at the request of the Ministry, and this established a sufficiently close relationship to create the employer's vicarious liability.

The following are features to be considered when assessing the second test of 'course of employment':

- An employer may be liable for authorized acts conducted in unauthorized ways (compare *Twine v Bean's Express Ltd* [1946] and *Rose v Plenty* [1976]).
- An employer may be liable for acts committed which are incidental to the employment (*Crook v Derbyshire Stone Ltd* [1956]).
- Where the employee has deviated from the task of their employment, the extent of the deviation will determine whether the employer is vicariously liable or not (*Storey v Ashton* [1869]).

Where an employee commits a criminal act in the course of their employment, the employer has been held jointly culpable (*Daniels v Whetstone Entertainments and Allender* [1962]). It is necessary to consider the closeness of the connection between the wrong committed by the employee and the nature of their employment, and to determine whether it is just and reasonable in those circumstances to hold the employer vicariously liable (*Lister v Hesley Hall* [2001]). In *Maga v Trustees of the Birmingham Archdiocese of the Roman Catholic Church* [2010], the Court of Appeal held that this liability extended to child abuse committed by a priest, through existence of a 'sufficiently close connection' between his actions and his employment. Similarly in *Mohamud v WM Morrison Supermarkets Plc* [2014], the brutal and unprovoked attack committed by an employee of Morrisons supermarket created the liability of the employer because this was an abuse of the job the employee was instructed to perform. It was connected with the job as the employee did have dealings with customers.

The Consumer Protection Act 1987

The CPA 1987 assists consumers when seeking damages against defects in products which have caused injury or caused damage, and adds to existing common law rights. The CPA 1987 makes such claims much easier as it imposes strict liability—negligence does not have to be proved. Liability is only removed if a defence can be made under the Act's provisions.

Requirements

The claimant must bring their claim within three years of awareness of the damage or defect in the product, and they must satisfy the following criteria:

- the product contained a defect;
- the claimant suffered damage;
- the damage was caused by the defect; and
- the defendant was either a producer, a marketer (own-brander), the first importer, or a supplier of the product.

The Occupiers' Liability Acts

There exist obligations (duties to take reasonable care) on occupiers of premises to both lawful visitors and to trespassers. The duty of care (a statutory duty rather than the common law duty which arises in negligence) is to ensure, as far as is reasonable, that the visitor will be safe in using the premises for the purposes for which they are invited to be there.

Premises have to be reasonably safe—assessed in light of the danger that the visitor was exposed to at the premises. In determining this danger, the test of reasonable foreseeability of the risk of injury to the (specific) claimant (such as for an adult or child) in the use, as would be reasonably expected, of the premises is adopted (*Tomlinson v Congleton BC* [2004]). The courts will also look at the potential gravity of the harm, the utility of the defendant's conduct, and the cost of taking precautions.

A distinction between the **Occupiers' Liability Acts (OLA) 1957 and 1984** is that the 1984 Act was more restrictive in providing that the duty of care to those other than the occupier's visitor was restricted to a danger that the occupier of the premises knows of, or ought to know exists. Further, the occupier must know or ought to know that the trespasser is likely to come onto their land.

Occupier

'Occupier' in the **OLA 1957 s 1(2)** refers to using the common law definition—the person who has control over the premises (*Wheat v Lacon* **[1966]**).

Duties to visitors

The **OLA 1957** requires that the occupier of premises takes reasonable care to ensure that a visitor to their premises will be reasonably safe.

A visitor is a person who comes onto premises with the express or implied permission of the occupier.

The lawful visitor may also become a trespasser if they wrongfully use the premises (*Owners of SS Otarama v Manchester Ship Canal Co* [1926]).

The duty to take care is tested in accordance with the **Compensation Act 2006 ss 1 and 2**. The requirement in **OLA 1957 s 2(2)** that the visitor is reasonably safe for the purposes for which they have been invited does not remove the expectation of the person to exercise common sense and to take care of their own safety (*Lewis v Six Continents Plc* **[2005]**).

> ### ✔️ Looking for extra marks?
>
> Always consider in your deliberations to an essay or problem question that the obligation to protect visitors is determined in regard to the actual, not hypothetical, visitor. For example, warning signs appropriate to adults may not be adequate with regard to minors, and a visitor to premises undertaken as part of their job is deemed to have a better understanding of the inherent risks in the pursuit of that activity than would an 'ordinary' visitor.

Claims under the **OLA 1957** may be made in respect of personal injury, losses, or damage to property. The occupier may raise the defence of contributory negligence (as it is fault-based liability) and *volenti* to an action, but simply because the claimant agrees to a notice or contract term that purports to exclude the defendant's liability will not amount to acceptance of the inherent risk (**UCTA 1977 s 2(3)**).

Duties to non-visitors

The **OLA 1984** broadened the common law duty owed to trespassers. It imposes a duty of care on the occupier to trespassers and persons entering land without the permission or consent of the occupier (who are known as non-visitors).

The obligation on the occupier is to take reasonable care to ensure that the non-visitor is not injured due to any danger on the premises (**OLA 1984 s 1(4)**). The obligation may be removed through adequate warnings and protective measures being taken to identify (and minimize) the risk. The occupier owes the duty where (**OLA 1984 s 1(3)**):

- they are aware of the danger, or ought reasonably to be aware that a danger exists;
- they must be aware, or have reasonable grounds to believe, that the non-visitor is in the vicinity of the danger and may enter the premises (regardless of any lawful right to be in the area); and
- the danger must be of a type that it is reasonable to expect the occupier to protect against.

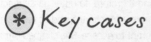

(✱) *Key cases*

Case	Facts	Principle
Barnett v Chelsea and Kensington Hospital Management Committee [1969] 1 QB 428	A man sought medical treatment following a bout of vomiting. A nurse, following consultation with a doctor, informed the man to go home and seek assistance from his general practitioner if his symptoms did not improve. The man died later that day from arsenic poisoning.	The courts established the 'but for' test. Here, as the man would have died anyway due to the concentration of arsenic in his body, irrespective of medical intervention, the claim had to fail. The failure to examine him did not cause the man's death.
Caparo Industries Plc v Dickman and Others [1990] 2 AC 605	In the takeover of a company, the claimants relied on information provided by the auditors for the purposes of the company's annual accounts. The accounts were negligently prepared and this led to the claimants suffering economic loss.	The case involved pure economic loss but the claim failed as the accounts had been prepared on the basis of a legal requirement—not to provide investment advice. There existed no 'special relationship' between the parties that would have established proximity between them.
Hedley Byrne & Co v Heller [1963] 2 All ER 575	A company approached a bank to verify the creditworthiness of a third company. A negligent reference was provided identifying the company as being creditworthy when in reality they were not. Credit was advanced on the basis of the reference and the claimants suffered loss when this money was never repaid.	Whilst liability for pure economic loss is very difficult to establish successfully, defendants who have made negligent misstatements may be held liable where a 'special relationship of proximity' exists between the parties, and breach and causation are also established.

Exam questions

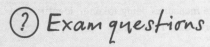

(?) Exam questions

Problem question

Redmount Borough Council is responsible for the operation of the local railway station. Marala and her husband arrived at the station at 4.30am to take the 4.50am train for their journey. Before the train arrived, Marala went to the toilet. She entered the cubicle and locked the door. When she attempted to vacate the cubicle, she found the lock had broken and she was trapped inside. It was later discovered that the Council had received complaints about the lock being in poor repair and that it was sticking, but the Council did not repair it.

Marala did not have a mobile phone with her. She shouted for her husband to help her, and for the attendant, but no one came to assist her. The train station was deserted and therefore no other passengers were available to help. Having been trapped in the cubicle for approximately 15 minutes, and as her train was leaving imminently, Marala considered her only option was to attempt to escape. She climbed onto the toilet bowl and managed to pull herself up to the top of the door, but realized that she was not in a sufficiently fit physical condition to climb all the way over the door. As she began to lower herself down, she placed her foot, and her weight, onto the toilet roll holder affixed to the wall. When she had put almost all of her weight on the holder, it spun round and Marala slipped down to the floor, injuring her back and leg.

Marala required hospital treatment. She has a pre-existing medical condition which was made considerably worse following the fall. Further, Marala missed her journey on the train as planned. This was to a five-star hotel and spa which she and her husband had booked for a one-week stay. The cost of the hotel was £1,500, which was offered on a non-refundable contract.

Tasks:

1. Advise Marala if the Council has any responsibility for her injuries under the tort of negligence.

2. Explain the 'eggshell skull rule' and how this may apply to Marala.

3. In relation to a defence available to the Council, explain the defence of contributory negligence and whether it will apply here.

4. Explain the issue of 'remoteness of loss' and how it would apply to Marala's possible claim for the loss of her holiday.

An outline answer is included at the end of the book.

Essay question

How has the law developed in holding employers liable for the criminal acts of their employees? Do you agree with the direction of the courts in this respect?

◯ Online Resources

To see an outline answer to this question log on to www.oup.com/lawrevision/

#7

Employment I: employment status, equal pay, and equality

Key facts

- Individuals may be engaged as workers, but their employment status will most commonly be as an employee (employed under a contract *of* service) or independent contractor (employed under a contract *for* services).

- Employment status is significant in relation to the rights and obligations each type of contract has for the individual and employer.

- Given the lack of an adequate statutory definition, the common law has developed tests to identify employment status (mutuality of obligations, evidence of an employer's right to control, and whether the individual was engaged in business on their own account).

- Employees and people employed personally to perform work under a contract are protected against various forms of discrimination. Some of these also apply before employment.

Introduction

Employment status is a crucial element to identify the rights and responsibilities of the parties to an employment relationship. The employment status enjoying the most comprehensive rights is that of an **employee**. There also exist workers, employee shareholders, and finally, at the opposite end of the employment status spectrum (and enjoying the fewest employment rights), **independent contractors**. It is only necessary to establish if an individual is an employee or independent contractor where they are seeking access to a right which is dependent upon 'employee' status, or to identify obligations imposed on an employer. Further, the common law tests have developed to assist in this matter where there is disagreement between the individual and the employer about the individual's status.

Some rights, such as to receive the National Minimum Wage, apply to a broader set of individuals simply due to the significance of the right and the need to cover as many workers as is reasonable (generally those who have a contract of employment and/or are employed personally to perform the tasks).

Workers

There are many forms of working relationship. Some individuals may be held as independent contractors, others are deemed employees. Further, there are those who work under no contract at all. Workers are those individuals who, whilst not employees, undertake to personally provide the work or service for the employer. Note that commonly in assessments individuals will (normally) fall under one of the two predominant categories—independent contractors and employees.

Employee shareholders

From 1 September 2013, the status of employee shareholder (**Employment Rights Act (ERA) 1996 s 205A**) had been created (the **Growth and Infrastructure Act 2013**). Under such a contract, the individual operates as an employee shareholder with either the employer's company or the employer's parent company.

Significantly, the individual had to be provided with shares in the company with a minimum value of £2,000 (which must be fully paid up and for which the individual must not be charged).

Employee shareholders legally waive their rights to protections in the following areas:

a) Unfair dismissal (unless the dismissal is on the basis of an automatically unfair reason, is in breach of the **Equality Act 2010**, or is to do with a health and safety ground);

b) Statutory redundancy payment;

c) The statutory right to request flexible working (except in the two-week period following the return from parental leave); and

d) Statutory rights relating to requests for time off to undertake training.

The **Finance Bill 2017** withdrew the Capital Gains Tax exemption and the Income Tax reliefs in respect of shares received when entering into most Employee Shareholder Status agreements. Agreements entered into before 1 December 2016, or before 2 December 2016 (where the independent advice was received before 1:30pm on 23 November 2016) retain the tax benefits. However, this means that no further Employee Shareholders will be created. Existing Employee Shareholders will continue to enjoy the benefits of that status.

Employment status

A legislative definition is provided in the **ERA 1996 s 230** but this is deliberately broad and is supplemented by the common law tests (which advanced over time). As such the evolution of the tests represents a historical development of the courts' thinking—reflecting the increased diversity and complexity of modern forms of employment.

Revision tip

Note that no one test is conclusive of employment status and the tribunal is given much discretion in concluding the individual's status according to the evidence presented.

The common law tests include:

- the right to control test: evidence of control exercisable by the employer;
- the integration/organization test: whether the individual is integrated into the workforce;
- the mixed test: as developed in the case *Ready Mixed Concrete* [1968] (the mixed test);
- whether the individual is 'in business on their own account';
- the existence of **mutuality of obligations**.

Revision tip

Always begin your application of the law with reference to *Montgomery v Johnson Underwood* [2001]. You should identify the requirement for an element of control and mutuality of obligations to be present before moving to the *Ready Mixed Concrete* tests.

Important initial factors

Whilst tests exist to assist in identifying whether an individual is an employee or independent contractor, the tribunal is entitled to give whatever weight it thinks appropriate to the various factors (*Hall v Lorimer* [1993]). For example, in some instances tribunals consider that the individual paying their own tax and National Insurance is indicative of working as an independent contractor (although unlikely to be singularly conclusive), whilst in other cases such payments have not prevented the individual being held as an employee (*Ferguson v John Dawson & Partners* [1976]).

The mixed test

The courts expanded on the control and integration tests and added further questions that would assist in identifying employment status.

Ready Mixed Concrete v Minister of Pensions and National Insurance [1968] 2 WLR 775

Ready Mixed Concrete employed drivers and their employment status had to be determined for tax purposes. Mackenna J identified three questions to assist in determining employment status:

1. the servant agrees that, in consideration of a wage or other remuneration, he will provide his own work and skill in the performance of some service for his master;
2. he agrees, expressly or impliedly, that in the performance of that service he will be subject to the other's control in a sufficient degree to make that other master;
3. the other provisions of the contract are consistent with its being a contract of service.

Individual 'in business on their own account'

The essence of an employee is their dependence on the employer, whilst the independent contractor invests in the business, undertakes a financial risk, often provide their own tools and also has the ability to benefit in the business' success (*Lee Ting Sang v Chung Chi-Keung* [1990]).

✅ Looking for extra marks?

The 'business on their own account' test appears to be appropriate and sensible, but it is fraught with practical difficulties. How do you differentiate between an independent contractor who has a financial risk in their business (prospectively buying materials/stock etc) with an employee who is, for example, a stock broker who earns the bulk of their income through commission payments? They both undertake financial risk and can gain or suffer losses depending on their work. A critical examination of this test can lead to a significantly improved answer in comparison with what may be possible by simply describing the test in an answer.

Mutuality of obligations

An essential feature of the employment relationship (see Table 7.1) is the existence of mutuality of obligations (*Market Investigations Ltd v Minister of Social Security* [1969]). Here the employee has an obligation to be available for work and the employer has a corresponding duty to provide work or wages (*Carmichael v National Power Plc* [2000]).

✅ Looking for extra marks?

Mutuality of obligations offers better students opportunities to demonstrate their critical understanding of the topic of employment status. Use *Nethermere (St Neots) Ltd v Gardiner and Taverna* [1984] and *O'Kelly and Others v Trusthouse Forte plc* [1984] to critique the broad and narrow approaches to the application of mutuality. Further, given that mutuality of obligations is not a test used exclusively in employment (relational) contracts, why should it be so crucial to determine employment status?

Table 7.1 Features of the employment relationship

	Features of the Employment Relationship					
Employment status	Control exercisable by the employer **(essential)**	Integrated into the business	A contract of personal service (eg no ability to subcontract)	On business on own account **(fundamental)**	Mutuality of obligations **(essential)**	Tax and NI taken at source **(indicative not conclusive)**
Employee	Yes	Yes (but difficult to define)	Yes	No	Yes	Yes
Independent contractor	No	Not necessarily	No	Yes	No	No

Label used

A label of employee/independent contractor is persuasive but not conclusive, and the tribunal will look to the true nature of the employment relationship, having heard all the evidence (*Ferguson v John Dawson & Partners* [1976]).

Pimlico Plumbers & Charlie Mullins v Gary Smith [2018] UKSC 29

Smith was a plumber who was engaged by the appellant between 2005 and 2011. Following suffering a heart attack in 2011, Smith claimed he was unfairly or wrongfully dismissed on 3 May 2011. The appellant argued that as Smith was an independent contractor (labelled a 'sub contracted employee') he had no right to claim unfair dismissal. The Supreme Court held that Smith was a worker and not a self-employed contractor. Pimlico exercised control over Smith. Smith had an obligation to perform the work personally (with a very restrictive right of substitution) and Pimlico was not a client or customer of his.

Revision tip

Always remember that due to the largely unscientific approach to the application of the common law tests to the facts presented at tribunal, and the policy/vitiating factors applied by some employment judges, second-guessing how a tribunal will determine employment status is difficult. This is not to say that this will inevitably happen, but it is worthy of consideration as tribunals have clearly demonstrated the use of vitiating factors in their awards.

Written particulars of employment

Employers are obliged to provide employees with a copy of the written particulars of employment within two months of the start of employment (**ERA 1996 s 1**). This document is not the contract of employment (eg because of the various implied terms in the contract), but it includes many of the features of the contract (*Systems Floors v Daniel* [1981]).

However, note that at **ERA 1996 s 2(6)** the right to written particulars exists even where the person's employment is terminated before the expiry of two months' time. In *Stefanko and others v Maritime Hotel Ltd* [2018] the Employment Appeal Tribunal (EAT) held that waiting staff engaged for only six weeks were entitled to receive the particulars and when these were not given, the claimant was entitled to an increased award (damages) as provided for in the **Employment Act 2002 s 38**. An exception does prevent the requirement for written particulars to be granted to a person who has worked for the employer for a period of less than one month.

An important update to this area of law will apply from 6 April 2020. The **Employment Rights (Employment Particulars and Paid Annual Leave) (Amendment) Regulations 2018** require that written particulars be provided from the first day of employment. The **Employment Rights (Miscellaneous Amendments) Regulations 2019** extends the right to written particulars to workers (and not just employees as is the current law).

Revision tip

Implied terms may be used as a discretely examinable topic due to the obligations they place on the parties and because it allows a discussion of their effects on what many employees may believe to be their contract of employment—namely the written particulars. Do not simply list the implied terms but flesh out an answer with reference to the case law and consider that many implied terms are conditions, not warranties.

Implied terms in contracts of employment

Implied terms exist in contracts of employment on the same basis as is applicable under contract law (see Chapter 4). Terms are implied as a matter of law and fact and may be found in various sources including:

- statutes (such as a pay equality clause in employment through the **Equality Act (EA) 2010**);
- customs (*Sagar v Ridehalgh* [1931]);
- works handbooks (enabling an employer to establish terms affecting large numbers of individuals instead of incorporating these terms into each employee's contract).

The EAT held there is an implied term that an employer will not dismiss an employee for incapability if that would prevent entitlement to long-term disability benefits. This limits the express contractual right to terminate on notice if it would frustrate the contractual entitlement to long term disability benefits (*Awan v ICTS UK Ltd* [2018]).

Equality law

The **EA 2010** affects groups wider than just employees and employers, but as the focus of this chapter is on employment, the functioning of the **EA 2010** is limited to these groups.

Protected characteristics

For an individual to be protected under the **EA 2010**, they must possess (or in some cases be associated with a person with) a characteristic identified in the legislation. The specific characteristics protected are:

- Age (s 5).
- Disability (s 6): an individual possesses a disability where they have a physical or mental impairment that has a substantial and long-term effect on their ability to carry out normal day-to-day activities. Employers are required to make 'reasonable adjustments' to accommodate individuals with a disability.

For the purposes of disability discrimination, an employer will not be treated as knowing that an employee has a disability where medical evidence wrongly identifies the employee as not being disabled (*Donelien v Liberata UK* [2018]).

The employer is required to make reasonable adjustments for 'actual' persons with a disability rather than hypothetical persons, or to anticipate the needs of persons with disabilities. In *Kaltoft v Municipality of Billund* [2014] an individual's weight (their BMI categorizing the individual as obese) was raised as a ground for disability. Ultimately this is not a free-standing aspect of equality law (it is tied to disability and the effects of obesity rather than obesity itself—see *Taylor v Ladbrokes Betting & Gaming Ltd* [2016]) but is a factor employers should be mindful of. Ensure you compare the social and medical models when determining whether a breach of the EU and domestic laws on disability discrimination has occurred.

✅ *Looking for extra marks?*

H J Heinz Co Ltd v Kenrick [2002] and *Rothwell v Pelikan Hardcopy Scotland Ltd* [2006] identified that an employer's failure to enquire about an employee's medical condition, which led to his dismissal on health grounds, constituted a breach of the (then relevant law) **Disability Discrimination Act 1995**.

- Gender reassignment (s 7): an individual who proposes to undergo, is currently undergoing, or who has undergone a process of reassigning their sex is protected against discrimination on the basis of this protected characteristic. Medical procedures are no longer necessary to qualify for protection—the individual must simply live permanently as the reassigned gender.

Equality law

****

- Marriage and civil partnership (s 8): single people are not protected.
- Pregnancy and maternity (ss 72–76).
- Race (s 9): this term includes 'colour; nationality; and ethnic or national origins'. The protected characteristic applies to a person of a particular racial group or persons of the same racial group.
- Religion or belief (s 10): protection against discrimination is provided on the basis of an individual's choice of religion, religious beliefs (or non-belief), or other similar philosophical belief—be that a real or perceived belief.

In *Eweida & Others v UK* [2013], national courts had to examine the EA 2010 in conjunction with the European Convention on Human Rights in respect of employers' dress codes at work. The Court of Justice of the European Union has also been active on identifying the extent of discrimination—especially in cases dealing with the wearing of Islamic headscarves at work. In Case C-157/15 *Achbita, Centrum voor Gelijkheid van kansen en voor racismebestrijding v G4S Secure Solutions* [2017] an employer's unwritten rule that prohibited employees from wearing visible signs of their political, philosophical, or religious beliefs in the workplace was not a breach of the Equal Treatment in Employment and Occupation Directive (Council Directive 2000/78/EC). The employer's aim was to promote a sense of neutrality and this legitimate aim was applied in a proportionate manner. Significantly, Achbita interacted with customers and this was directly associated with the purpose of achieving the aim of the employer.

Note that there is no discrimination based on philosophical belief where the employee is the only person to hold such a belief (here it was the sanctity of copyright law!—*Gray v Mulberry* [2018]).

- Sex (s 11).
- Sexual orientation (s 12): an individual's sexual orientation is their orientation towards persons of the same sex (homosexual), opposite sex (heterosexual), or both sexes (bisexual).

It is not directly discriminatory for a Christian baker to refuse to bake a cake containing a message in support of gay marriage (*Lee v Ashers Baking Company Ltd* [2018]). The Supreme Court held that the baker's refusal was not due to the sexual orientation of the customer nor was there evidence of associative discrimination. Simply because the message on the cake had something to do with the sexual orientation of some people was not sufficient to meet the threshold of discrimination.

An Occupational Qualification defence exists where being of a particular sexual orientation is:

- a genuine and determining occupational requirement;
- it is proportionate to those ends; and
- in the case of organized religions, where the sexual orientation contradicts the beliefs of the members of the particular religion.

Prohibited conduct

Having established that the claimant possesses, is associated with a person who possesses, or where the defendant perceives the claimant to possess one of the characteristics listed, the defendant will breach the individual's rights where they commit or permit a form of prohibited conduct to take place.

The types of behaviour which constitute prohibited conduct are:

- Direct discrimination: applies to all of the protected characteristics. It occurs where a person (eg, in this context, the employer) treats another (eg an employee) less favourably because of their protected characteristic than they would a person who does not possess the characteristic. Direct discrimination applies to actual, associated, or perception-based forms of less favourable treatment.

Generally, direct discrimination cannot be justified. However, exceptions do exist where discriminatory behaviour is necessary or a common sense approach is needed.

It is permissible to treat an individual less favourably on the basis of their age where the behaviour is a proportionate means of achieving a legitimate aim.

It is permissible to treat an individual with a disability more favourably than a person without the disability.

- Associative discrimination: applies to the protected characteristics except marriage and civil partnership, and pregnancy and maternity. It allows an individual protection due to the characteristic of a person with whom they are associated.

- Perception-based discrimination: applies to the protected characteristics except marriage and civil partnership, and pregnancy and maternity. It allows an individual protection against discrimination on the basis of a protected characteristic which they do not possess, but the person discriminating perceives they possess.

- Indirect discrimination: applies to the protected characteristics except marriage and civil partnership, and pregnancy and maternity (although it may apply to the protected characteristic of indirect sex discrimination). It occurs where a seemingly neutral provision, criterion, or practice is applied (eg to a job advertisement) which disadvantages people possessing a protected characteristic and cannot be objectively justified as a proportionate means of achieving a legitimate aim.

Equality law

****

The legitimate aim (where the employer puts this forward as a defence to the indirect discrimination) must be a genuine and objective business/economic need, but it should not be based on 'merely' reducing the costs of the organization.

An act of indirect discrimination may be justified where imposing the 'offending' condition or provision is a proportionate means of achieving a legitimate aim (*Panesar v Nestle Ltd* [1980]).

> *Revision tip*
>
> Employers are not permitted to use the argument of a 'legitimate aim' to segregate workers based on, for example, their race, or they face committing an act of discrimination.

The Court of Appeal in *R (on the application of Elias) v Secretary of State for Defence* [2005] identified the following questions to be considered by a tribunal in determining the legitimacy of whether the provision, criterion, or practice was proportionate:

- Is the objective to be achieved sufficiently important to justify limiting a right provided by the law?
- Is the measure(s) taken by the employer associated with the objective to be achieved?
- Is the measure(s) no more onerous than is necessary to achieve the objective?

- Harassment: applies to the protected characteristics except marriage and civil partnership, and pregnancy and maternity. The harassment may be sexual harassment, amount to less favourable treatment because of the sexual harassment, or it may be related to sex or gender reassignment; or it may be related to a person's protected characteristic.

> *Revision tip*
>
> The word 'harassment' refers to a series of actions but remember a one-off act may be sufficiently serious and enable a claim of harassment (*Bracebridge Engineering Ltd v Darby* [1990]).

- Victimization: victimization (eg intimidation of the individual, unfair pressure, etc) applies where an individual is subjected to a detriment on the basis that they have performed, or the employer believes they intend to perform, what is called a 'protected act'. A protected act, for example, includes initiating proceedings in the EA 2010. A comparator is unnecessary in victimization cases.

Remedies

The claim for discrimination must be brought within three months of the discriminatory act (or it having ended) although tribunals have the power to extend this time limit where they feel it just and equitable to do so.

Following a successful finding of discrimination, the three remedies that a tribunal is empowered to award are:

- declare the rights of the complainant;
- award damages (of which there is no statutory-imposed ceiling and may include the damage suffered to the claimant's feelings (*O'Donoghue v Redcar BC* [2001])—even psychiatric injury);
- make a recommendation that the employer eliminates/reduces the effect of the discrimination for all employees, not just the claimant.

Employers' liability for acts of discrimination

An employer has a responsibility to their employees, and where the employer is approached by an employee who complains that they were subject to a discriminatory act or harassment from an employee or agent of the employer, the employer has a duty to take reasonable action to prevent its recurrence (*Pearce v Governing Body of Mayfield School* [2003]).

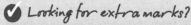 **Looking for extra marks?**

Croft v Royal Mail Group Plc [2003] held that if the steps required to prevent discrimination against an employee involve disproportionate expense and trouble, or may prove to be counter-productive or unlikely to achieve a positive result, the employer will not be at fault for failing to pursue them.

Equal pay

The **EA 2010 s 66** implies an equality clause in every contract of employment. Therefore, it is unlawful to pay men and women differently because of their sex unless the employer can demonstrate objective grounds for the difference in pay. Further, equality in pay applies to all employers, regardless of their size, and to part-time and full-time workers equally. There is no qualification period required to benefit from protection in this area of law.

Pay is the key issue and it includes not only the wages an individual receives, but all the terms and conditions involving remuneration—occupational benefits, sick pay, pension contributions, etc. Courts and tribunals will consider each element of the contract separately to identify any discrepancies in pay.

The comparator

As an equal pay claim must be of discriminatory pay on the basis of the claimant's sex, a comparator of the opposite sex must be used. In most cases an actual comparator who is working for the same employer, at the same time, and at the same place as the claimant must be presented. However, any cases of equal pay brought after 1 October 2010 and involving direct gender pay discrimination may involve use of a hypothetical comparator. In *Asda Stores Ltd v Brierley & Ors* [2016], the Court of Appeal held that despite geographical and organizational distinctions between two sets of workers, where a single source was the reason for the alleged disparity in pay, they were in the same employment for the purposes of the law.

The comparator may not be the claimant's successor (*Walton Centre for Neurology v Bewley* [2008]), although their predecessor may be used (*Macarthys Ltd v Smith* [1980]).

Head of claim

There are three 'heads' of claim that may be used in an equal pay action—depending on the available/appropriate comparator. The claimant must choose one as the basis for their claim:

- Like work: this applies to situations where the claimant and their comparator are doing like or similar work—minor differences of no real significance are ignored (**s 65(1)(b)**— *Electrolux Ltd v Hutchinson* [1977]).

- Work rated as equivalent: where an employer has performed a job evaluation study (which must be analytical and objective) and has provided pay on the basis of the results—to aid transparency, for example—the claimant or employer may use the results to bring/defend a claim for equal pay (**s 65(4)(b)**). To be effective, the claimant's and the comparator's jobs must have been involved in the study and it must have been conducted in the place where they are both employed.

Where the comparator's job is rated lower than that of the claimant, yet the comparator is paid more, this will not prevent the comparator being suitable for the purposes of a claim (*Bainbridge v Redcar & Cleveland BC* [2007]).

- Work of equal value: in the event that the most appropriate comparator to the claimant is doing a different job, and the employer has not conducted a job evaluation study, a claim may be made on the basis that both the claimant and comparator are performing jobs providing equal value to the employer. Value in this context refers to factors such as responsibility, skill, qualifications, effort, decision-making, etc.

An equal value claim is possible even where a 'token' man is employed in the same job as the claimant (see *Pickstone v Freemans Plc* [1988]).

The benefit of this head of claim is that the claimant may use a comparator performing a different job to themselves, and the assessment is on the basis of the claimant's and comparator's contributions and value added to the business.

All the individual terms and conditions of the contract have to be equalized, rather than looking at the broad aspects of the contracts of the claimant and comparator (see *Hayward v Cammell Laird Shipbuilders* [1988]).

Defences to a claim

An employer, following a successful prima facie finding of a difference in pay between the claimant and comparator, may present a material factor defence. This is a tactic that may be used to avoid equalizing of the pay between the claimant and the comparator.

Such a defence must be that the 'material' difference in pay is not because of the sex of the claimant, but rather it can be objectively justified as a proportionate means of achieving a legitimate business aim. Examples of material factors include:

- responsibility (eg additional responsibilities undertaken by the comparator—*Shields v E Coomes Ltd* [1978]);

- market forces (eg where it is necessary to provide pay at different rates to entice workers from the private sector into the public sector—*Rainey v Greater Glasgow Health Board* [1987]);

- collective bargaining agreements (*Enderby v Frenchay Health Authority* [1994]);

- experience;

- regional variations: an employer may seek to justify differences in pay because the claimant's and comparator's work exist in different locations (*NAAFI v Varley* [1976]);

- **red-circle** agreements (*Snoxell v Vauxhall Motors Ltd* [1977]).

Time limits

A claim for equal pay may be made:

- at any time whilst the individual is engaged under a 'stable employment relationship' (*Preston v Wolverhampton Healthcare NHS Trust* [2001]); or

- within six months of the individual leaving the employment (and bringing a 'rolled-up' claim).

The claim can then be backdated (where applicable) for the previous six years.

Figure 7.1 demonstrates the stages of a claim for equal pay.

Gender pay gap reporting

The **Equality Act 2010 (Gender Pay Gap Information) Regulations 2017** provide that employers in Great Britain with at least 250 employees are required to publish information regarding differences in pay between male and female employees. Some public authorities will be exempt from this requirement—**Equality Act 2010 (Specific Duties and Public Authorities) Regulations 2017**.

Equal pay

****

Figure 7.1 Equal Pay Act—stages of claim

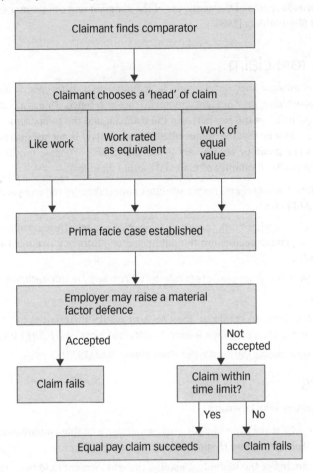

The reporting requirements apply to employees, workers, casual workers, and the self-employed (where they provide the services personally). An exception to the reporting requirements is where the employer does not have, nor is it reasonably practicable for them to collect, information on those individuals who are required to personally complete the work (workers and some self-employed individuals).

Employers have to publish:

- The mean and median pay differences between male and female 'full-time relevant employees.'
- The proportion of male and female 'relevant employees' who received bonus pay (assessed during the period of 12-months, ending with a snapshot on 5 April).

- The proportions of these 'relevant employees' in the lower, lower middle, upper middle, and upper quartile pay bands.

- However, overtime payments are excluded from the calculations.

Compliance

- The relevant information must be published within a 12-month period beginning with the 5 April snapshot date.

- The data must be signed off by a senior person in the organization and published on its website for a period of not less than three years. The data will have to be uploaded to a government-sponsored website.

- A failure to provide the data will be considered an 'unlawful act' that thereby enables the Equalities and Human Rights Commission to commence enforcement proceedings against the recalcitrant employer.

Employers may also provide a narrative or commentary on any differences and the data presented generally. This may include details of any pay gap to put the information in context, explain any difference in pay, and if so, what the employer plans to do to remedy the difference.

Discrimination against part-time workers

Part-time workers are not to be treated less favourably than their full-time counterparts (unless there is some objective reason for the distinction). The **Part-time Workers (Prevention of Less Favourable Treatment) Regulations 2000** provide part-time workers with the right to:

- the relevant proportion of pay;
- access to pension schemes;
- holiday leave;
- sick leave;
- maternity leave;
- training and access to promotion;

on a pro-rata basis, as for full-time workers.

Revision tip

Differences may exist between the full- and part-time workers with regards to overtime pay. The part-time workers would have to work beyond the 'normal' contracted hours of the full-time workers to benefit from this additional rate of pay.

Workers may compare each other's treatment to identify evidence of less favourable treatment where (s 2(4)):

- they are employed under the same type of contract;
- they are performing broadly similar work (and, where relevant, have similar levels of qualifications, skills, and experience); and
- the part-time worker and full-time worker are based at the same establishment; or where no full-time worker is based at the establishment who satisfies these criteria, works or is based at a different establishment and satisfies the criteria.

Discrimination against pregnant workers

It is automatically unfair dismissal to dismiss a woman for any reason due to her pregnancy. Discrimination against a pregnant worker is automatically direct sex discrimination and, as such, there is no defence or objective justification for the employer's action. Protection applies when the woman becomes pregnant and continues until the end of the maternity leave or until she returns to work if this is an earlier date (known as the protected period). Note that in *Lyons v DWP JobCentre Plus* [2014] the EAT held, following the authority in *Brown v Rentokil* [1998], that where a woman suffers a pregnancy-related illness which extends beyond the period of her maternity leave, the employer can consider the period of absence and compare the treatment of the claimant in such circumstances with how the employer would have treated a similarly ill man.

The **Parental Bereavement (Leave and Pay) Act 2018** has received Royal Assent and will be brought fully into force by April 2020. Whilst details of the rate of pay and so on have yet to be detailed in (forthcoming) Regulations, the Act does provide a right to two weeks' time off work for employees whose child under the age of 18 has died.

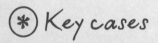

(✳) Key cases

Case	Facts	Principle
Carmichael v National Power Plc [2000] IRLR 43	Tour guides wished to gain protection afforded to employees although they worked 'as and when required'.	For employee status, a key element present is the mutuality of obligations—for the employer to provide work and the employee to be available for work or to accept it.
Ready Mixed Concrete v Minister of Pensions and National Insurance [1968] 2 WLR 775	Drivers for the company had to be determined as employees or independent contractors for tax purposes.	The three 'Ready Mixed' tests were established to assist in identifying employment status.

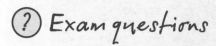

(?) Exam questions

Problem question

The Church of the One True God is a charity of the Christian faith that provides help and assistance for homeless people, including running soup kitchens and advice services. The charity wishes to appoint a new head chef to facilitate the expansion of this service to a wider region and prepares an advertisement of the post which includes the statement that 'practising Christians are preferred'.

Ahmed is friends with Susan, who works at the charity as an administrator. Ahmed is a Muslim and spoke with some of his friends (also of the Muslim faith) about the job, but they were dissuaded from applying. Despite this, Ahmed, in part due to encouragement from Susan, did apply but was not shortlisted for an interview despite having previous experience and being well qualified to undertake the responsibilities. Ahmed told Susan of this. Susan was very annoyed at what she considered was racism and she made a complaint to the Equality and Human Rights Commission and informed her local paper, which ran the story as a feature. Susan was summarily dismissed on the ground of misconduct.

In a further development at the charity, Mark, who has been employed as a fundraiser for five years, has recently been subjected to homophobic comments and jokes regarding his perceived sexual orientation due to his 'posh' accent. Mark is unhappy with the comments and the jokes made at his expense and he has raised the issue with his manager, but the manager refuses to take any action as he considers this as mere harmless workplace 'banter'. Since the meeting with his manager, Mark has found homophobic literature on his desk and it has also been pinned to the staff noticeboard.

Advise the parties as to their rights and responsibilities.

An outline answer is included at the end of the book.

Essay question

The nature of the common law tests used to establish employment status has enabled employers effectively to prevent many workers from accessing protective employment rights. This is likely to be exacerbated in the current economic climate. As a consequence, it is necessary for parliamentary action to remedy this significant deficiency in industrial relations.

Assess this statement and critically comment on the limitations of the common law tests.

● Online Resources

To see an outline answer to this question log on to www.oup.com/lawrevision/

#8

Employment II: termination— wrongful dismissal, unfair dismissal, and redundancy

Key facts

- Dismissals with the correct notice period will be deemed fair at common law. Summary dismissals (without notice) may be fair where justified by the employer.

- To avoid a successful claim of unfair dismissal, the employer should identify one of the potentially fair reasons to dismiss, conduct a reasonable investigation, and follow the Advisory, Conciliation and Arbitration Service (ACAS) code of practice in determining whether to dismiss/ discipline the employee.

- The **Employment Rights Act (ERA) 1996** provides for 'automatically' unfair reasons to dismiss an employee. As such the tribunal does not assess the fairness of the employer's decision to dismiss (as it would generally in cases alleging unfair dismissal).

- The primary remedy for a wrongful dismissal is a damages payment, whereas the remedies for unfair dismissal include compensation (damages), reinstatement, and re-engagement.

- Redundancy, a potentially fair reason to dismiss, occurs when an undertaking closes or where the employee's labour becomes surplus to the needs of the undertaking.

- Redundancy payments are calculated in the same way as the basic award in an unfair dismissal claim.

- Employers have a duty to consult with the workforce or their representatives with regard to any possible collective redundancy situations.

Introduction

Employees have the statutory right not to be unfairly dismissed and the **ERA 1996** identifies the criteria to be satisfied in order for the employee to gain protection. The common law also protects against **wrongful dismissal**, and the common law has provided tests and guidance as to situations involving a breach of an employment contract. Further, it is important to identify which of these actions (if the individual qualifies for both) should be pursued as each has its own advantages and disadvantages.

Finally, this chapter outlines redundancy situations. As this is governed by statute, it is necessary to appreciate the obligations imposed on the employer to adopt fair procedures.

Termination of employment

It is important to note that simply because a contract of employment has come to an end it does not necessarily result in a dismissal, or indeed that if it is a dismissal, that it is actionable. It is necessary to consider the qualifications required to plead unfair dismissal, wrongful dismissal, or redundancy, and also to consider which remedy may be most appropriate to the claimant.

Common law—wrongful dismissal

A wrongful dismissal occurs where the worker's contract of employment has been brought to an end contrary to the terms of the contract. This is generally seen where the worker has been summarily dismissed (dismissed without notice) and the employer has no justification for it. Gross misconduct may justify a **summary dismissal**.

Revision tip

The following facts should make you think about the possibility of a wrongful dismissal claim:

- where the individual does not have 'employee status';
- where the individual has been dismissed without any notice/the correct notice period;
- where an individual has been dismissed during a fixed-term contract and the contract does not contain provision for early termination.

Notice periods

In the absence of any contractual provision, the **ERA 1996 s 86** provides for the notice periods for termination of the employment contract shown in Table 8.1.

Remedies

As this is a contractual dispute, the damages awarded will attempt to place the injured party in the position in which they would have been had the contract not been breached. A damages payment includes the lost income due for the notice period. In a fixed-term contract with no

Termination of employment

****

Table 8.1 Notice periods for termination of employment

Period of employment	Notice period applicable
Less than 1 month	None
More than 1 month but less than 2 years	1 week
More than 2 years but less than 12 years	Maximum of 12 weeks (1 week for every year worked)
More than 12 years	12 weeks

early termination clause, the damages that may be claimed are the balance of the contract (*Addis v Gramophone Co Ltd* [1909]).

Damages are not subject to a statutory maximum.

Exceptionally, the courts may award an injunction, particularly where this will prevent a dismissal that attempts to circumvent a statutory right (*Irani v South West Hampshire Health Authority* [1985]).

> ✔ **Looking for extra marks?**
>
> A claim of wrongful dismissal may be advantageous for an individual whose damages (such as the contractual notice period) are likely to exceed the maximum allowed under a claim of unfair dismissal. Always consider the terms of the worker's contract in making your decision.

Where the worker has been wrongfully dismissed, they are under a duty to limit (mitigate) their losses. This 'encourages' the worker to seek alternative work as opposed to allowing the damages to continue to mount (*Brace v Calder* [1895]). The approach to be taken with regards to mitigation, from the Employment Appeal Tribunal (EAT) in *Cooper Contracting Ltd v Lindsey* [2015], is: 1) the burden of proof when submitting evidence rests with the wrongdoer rather than the claimant; 2) the claimant must have acted unreasonably and assessment of this requirement is objective (and based on a question of fact); and 3) simply because the individual did not accept a better paid job when available this will not automatically result in a conclusion of failure to mitigate.

After discovered reasons

The fairness of an employer's decision to dismiss a worker is assessed on the basis of the beliefs held at the time of the dismissal (*British Home Stores v Burchell* [1978]). However, if the employer dismisses the worker, and later discovers evidence that proves that the worker was in fact guilty of the alleged conduct, this evidence will be accepted by the court and can justify a dismissal as lawful—*Boston Deep Sea Fishing and Ice Co v Ansell* (1888).

How an employer may defeat a claim

Where the employer provides the required notice period, they will avoid a wrongful dismissal claim. A fundamental breach of the contract by the worker will enable the employer to dismiss the worker without notice. Fundamental breaches are usually one-off acts of serious misconduct—gross misconduct, gross negligence, and so on (*Parr v Whitbread* [1990]). Note that in *Adesokan*, no conduct can actually amount to misconduct:

Adesokan v Sainsbury's Supermarkets Ltd [2017] EWCA Civ 22

The claimant, a regional manager for Sainsbury's, received information that a manager in the human resources department had issued an email with the intention of negatively interfering with a management consultation exercise. He knew of the email but took no action. Following a disciplinary hearing, his (in) action was considered to be grossly negligent, and was 'tantamount to gross misconduct'. As such, he was dismissed, which the Court of Appeal held as justified in these circumstances.

Statutory claim—unfair dismissal

Statute protects employees from being unfairly dismissed and provides various remedies for breach (**ERA 1996 s 94(1)**). Figure 8.1 identifies the stages involved in a claim of unfair dismissal.

Qualifications to claim unfair dismissal

The **ERA 1996** establishes that the following criteria are required to be satisfied by the claimant:

1. the individual must have 'employee' status;
2. they must have been continuously employed by the same employer for at least two years;
3. they must have been dismissed; and
4. the claim must be submitted to a tribunal within three months of the Effective Date of Termination (EDT).

Exceptions to these qualification criteria: the employee does not have to demonstrate that they have been dismissed where they claim 'constructive' dismissal; and the two years' continuous employment requirement is removed in situations involving 'automatically' unfair reasons.

Revision tip

Unless the claim involves an automatically unfair dismissal or constructive unfair dismissal, each of the qualifications must be satisfied otherwise the claimant's action cannot proceed. Use this four-stage test before moving on to consider the substantive and procedural aspects.

Termination of employment

****

Figure 8.1 Unfair dismissal

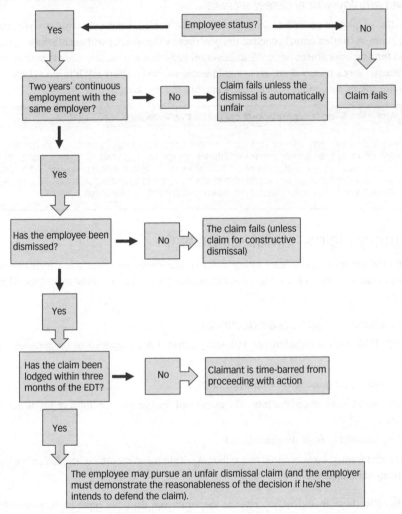

The effective date of termination

The EDT is assessed objectively (**ERA 1996 s 97**)—the parties cannot independently determine this date.

If a period of notice is given, the EDT will take effect when the notice period ends, not when the notice was given (**s 97(1)(a)**). If no notice is provided, the EDT takes effect from the date on which termination was effective (**s 97(1)(b)**).

Potentially fair reasons to dismiss

The **ERA 1996 s 98** outlines the reasons for which it may be fair, if reasonable on the facts, for the employer to dismiss the employee:

- the capability or qualifications of the employee (s 98(2)(a));
- the conduct of the employee (s 98(2)(b))—the employer is not required to prove that the employee was guilty of an alleged act of misconduct, rather, they must demonstrate reasonable grounds on which they held/maintained belief in the misconduct (*British Home Stores v Burchell* [1978]). The tests in *Burchell* may be less strictly adhered to when the facts of the issue are not in dispute between the parties (*Monie v Coral Racing Ltd* [1980]);
- that the employee was made redundant (s 98(2)(c))—usually involving an unfair selection for redundancy (*Williams v Compair Maxam Ltd* [1982]);
- that to continue the employment would amount to a contravention of a statute (s 98(2) (d))—such as where continuing to employ an individual would break the law (*Four Seasons Healthcare Ltd v Maughan* [2005]);
- some other substantial reason of a kind to justify dismissal of an employee holding the position which the employee held (s 98(1)(b)). Case law examples include: a homosexual man dismissed from his job at a residential holiday camp due to a potentially negative reaction from parents on discovering his sexuality (*Saunders v Scottish National Camps Association* [1980]); an employee's refusal to agree to the inclusion of a **restraint of trade clause** in his employment contract (*RS Components v Irwin* [1973]); and an employee's breach of the implied duty of trust and confidence (*Perkin v St George's Healthcare NHS Trust* [2005]).

✅ *Looking for extra marks?*

In *Scott v Richardson* [2005], the EAT held that the tribunal did not have to be satisfied that the commercial decision of the need for a reorganization was sound but, rather, the test was whether the employer believed it to be so.

Automatically unfair reasons to dismiss

The qualification of two years' continuous service to gain access to unfair dismissal protection is removed in certain circumstances. Whilst this list is not exhaustive, some of the most significant include:

- dismissals due to the pregnancy of the worker or any related illness (**ERA 1996 s 99**);
- dismissals due to a spent conviction under the **Rehabilitation of Offenders Act 1974**;
- dismissals due to trade union membership or activities (**Trade Union and Labour Relations (Consolidation) Act (TULRCA) 1992 s 238A(2)**);
- an unjustified dismissal as a result of a transfer of a business/change of service (**Transfer of Undertakings (Protection of Employment) Regulations (TUPE) 2006 reg 7**).

Time limits

A claim of unfair dismissal must be lodged at the Employment Tribunal within three months of the EDT. As this is a statutory right, there is little flexibility in this time limit for the tribunal to exercise, although it can be extended where it was not 'reasonably practicable' for the claimant to submit within this time frame (**ERA 1996 s 111**).

Procedures for a fair dismissal

ACAS, the Advisory, Conciliation and Arbitration Service, has produced a code of practice and procedural fairness identifying how the employer and employee should conduct themselves during grievance/disciplinary matters. The tribunal will consider whether the parties followed the code in determining the reasonableness of any action taken in such proceedings. The tribunal will be able to raise or lower any award by up to 25 per cent for an unreasonable failure to follow the code. The code is not law, but it is referred to by tribunals when assessing the reasonableness of an employer's decision to dismiss.

Early conciliation process

To facilitate greater use of conciliation to resolve disputes between an individual and their employer without recourse to an employment tribunal, the government introduced a scheme for early conciliation (**The Employment Tribunals (Early Conciliation: Exemptions and Rules of Procedure) (Amendment) Regulations 2014**). Here the employee and employer are obliged to have attempted to resolve the matter which has led to the dismissal prior to the employee being permitted to submit the claim to the employment tribunal. The parties have up to one calendar month, aided by ACAS, to reach an amicable resolution to the dispute. To protect the employee's potential claim, the three-month period in which their claim must be lodged at the tribunal is suspended during the conciliation process.

Reasonableness of a dismissal

It is necessary for the employer to demonstrate that they acted fairly in deciding to dismiss the employee. This burden of demonstrating reasonableness is neutral between the parties (**ERA 1996 s 98(4)**).

Reasonableness will include aspects such as the size of the business and the employer's access to assistance in the administration of discipline and investigations (the employee's work records, etc). Further, the employer will be expected to have treated workers consistently—for example, all workers previously engaged in similar actions which led to the employee's dismissal, had been dismissed. In determining reasonableness, the tribunal must not consider what action it would have taken (*Iceland Frozen Foods Ltd v Jones* [1982]). Hence, the tribunal will assess the evidence presented by the employer and whether their action fell into the band of reasonable responses.

The House of Lords, in the seminal case of *Polkey v A E Dayton Services* [1987], held that whether the employer had acted reasonably in dismissing an individual should be determined on the facts they had available when the decision was made and looking at what would have happened had the correct procedure been applied. A similar application of the law was recently confirmed in *Parker v The Chief Constable of Essex Police* [2018].

Constructive unfair dismissal

Constructive dismissal is a mechanism that enables a claim under unfair dismissal where the employee has not been 'dismissed' by the employer (one of the necessary qualifications to claim unfair dismissal). Rather, the employer has breached a fundamental term of the contract, or it can be shown that the employer no longer intends to be bound by an essential term(s), and the employee accepts the repudiation (**ERA 1996 ss 95(1)(c) and 136(1)(c)**—see Fig 8.2). Examples of such actions include:

Figure 8.2 Constructive dismissal

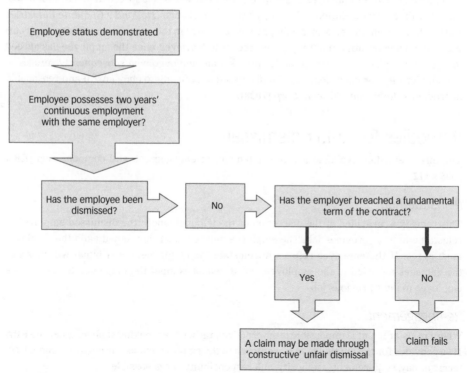

- the employer unilaterally reducing an employee's pay (*Industrial Rubber Products v Gillon* [1977]);
- failing to provide a safe and suitable working environment (*Waltons and Morse v Dorrington* [1997]);
- an unreasonable accusation of theft (*Robinson v Crompton Parkinson* [1978]);
- the harassment and bullying of workers (*Reed v Stedman* [1999]); and
- where the employer imposes a disciplinary penalty out of proportion to the offence that had been committed (*BBC v Beckett* [1983]).

In *Western Excavating v Sharp* [1978], the Court of Appeal identified the criteria by which constructive dismissal would be assessed. These were:

- the employer must have breached a term (express or implied), or had clearly established that they would not be bound by the contract;
- the term breached must have been an essential or fundamental term;
- the employee must have accepted the breach of the contract by the employer and acted to end the employment within a reasonable time.

Remember that an employee must take action quickly to claim constructive unfair dismissal or they may be viewed as having affirmed the change (*Holland v Glendale Industries Ltd* [1998]). The employee who is unhappy with a change in the contract must make some outward sign demonstrating that they do not accept it. However, once the employee has agreed to work to the changed contract 'under protest', an employee who subsequently refuses to work under the new conditions may be dismissed as refusing to obey lawful and reasonable instructions (*Robinson v Tescom Corp* [2008]).

Remedies for unfair dismissal

The three remedies available are reinstatement, re-engagement, and compensation (ERA 1996 s 112).

Reinstatement

This remedy is provided at the discretion of the tribunal where the dismissed employee is reinstated to their previous job. The employee must request this remedy and the employer must agree. If the employer refuses to reinstate the employee, the tribunal will increase the damages awarded to the employee, but it cannot compel the employer to restore the employee to their previous job.

Re-engagement

Where reinstatement is impossible or impractical, rather than making such an order the ERA 1996 provides for the employee to be returned to the employment as close to the same job (in terms of pay, requirements, seniority, and responsibility) as is possible.

Compensation

Compensation is provided by the tribunal on the basis of two elements—a basic award and a compensatory award (**ERA 1996 s 123(1)**). Under this section the tribunal will award a conventional sum of £250 by way of compensation for loss of a statutory right.

Basic award

This is the element of the award that is designed to reflect the employee's loss of pay between the time of the dismissal and the date of the tribunal's decision.

The calculation is based on **Employees Age** × **Length of Service** × **Weekly Gross Pay** (to the relevant maximum).

Compensatory award

This element of the award is not calculated to a strict formula and the tribunal has wide scope for assessing what is just and equitable in the circumstances. The award includes compensation for losses of overtime payments, tips, future losses, loss of accrued rights, and so on. The maximum award under the compensatory element is the lower of either (1) the maximum award entailed at the time of the claim—as of April 2019 £86,444 or (2) 12 months' gross pay (which figure excludes pension contributions, benefits paid by the employer, and any discretionary bonuses). However, where the employee has been dismissed for whistleblowing, some health and safety related reasons, or in the event of the dismissal being due to unlawful discrimination, the compensation remains uncapped.

As with the basic award, the compensation may be reduced where there was a contributory fault by the employee, or where the employee failed to mitigate their losses.

Additional award

The **ERA 1996 s 117** provides for additional compensation where, for example, the tribunal has ordered reinstatement or re-engagement and the employer has unreasonably refused to agree to the order. This award will be based on between 26 and 52 weeks' pay (at the tribunal's discretion).

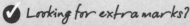 **Looking for extra marks?**

The remedies available for successful claims in wrongful dismissal and unfair dismissal are differentiated primarily on the individual being offered the previous job back (reinstatement/re-engagement). Always note the fact that reinstatement is the primary remedy in claims of unfair dismissal and there is a statutory cap on the damages that may be awarded. Wrongful dismissal only provides the remedy of damages (not reinstatement/re-engagement), although these are not subject to a statutory cap (see Table 8.2).

Termination of employment

****

Table 8.2 Comparison: Unfair Dismissal and Wrongful Dismissal

	Unfair Dismissal	Wrongful Dismissal
Source of the right	Statutory (ERA 1996).	Common Law (Contract).
Who may claim	Only available to employees.	Anyone with a contract to personally perform the work.
Minimum period of continuous employment required to access the right	Two years.	Immediate from the commencement of the contract.
Time limit within which a claim must be lodged	Three months.	Six years.
Where the claim is heard	Employment Tribunal.	County Court; High Court. A claim may be heard at an Employment Tribunal where the claim does not exceed £25,000.
Basis of the award	Compensation includes a basic award and a compensatory award to reflect ongoing and future losses.	Only covers the loss incurred for breach of the relevant notice period, or the balance of a fixed-term contract with no early termination clause.
Reasons for dismissal	s 98 ERA 1996 outlines potentially fair reasons for dismissal. The statute also identifies reasons for dismissal that will be automatically unfair.	The employer can choose any reason for dismissal. The stipulation is adherence to the notice period required under the contract.
Costs	Legal costs incurred in the action are now subject to award to the successful party.	Costs are more readily awarded in the County Court and High Court.
Fees	None to lodge the claim at the tribunal.	Legal fees for court applications to the County Court and High Court.
Discipline/dismissal procedures	ACAS code of practice and procedural fairness must be followed or the tribunal may raise/lower awards by up to 25%.	Any procedures provided by the employer in the contract must be adhered to.
After discovered reasons	Cannot make an unfair dismissal fair, but it may reduce any compensation awarded to a successful employee.	These may justify a dismissal, and if accepted by the court, will make a wrongful dismissal a fair dismissal.

	Unfair Dismissal	Wrongful Dismissal
Damages awarded	This is capped at (from 6 April 2019) £102,194—incorporating the basic and compensatory awards. However, either the lower of the statutory compensation or 12 months' gross pay will be awarded.	As this is a breach of contract claim there is no ceiling to the award of damages. It depends on the breach and the value of the contract.

Redundancy

Redundancy involves two broad scenarios. The employer may be closing the business and hence there is no work for the employee to do or the employer may have surplus labour overall following, for example, a reorganization or re-focus to the business (**ERA 1996 s 139**).

The tribunal is not allowed to assess the business need or rationale for the employer ending the business (*Moon v Homeworthy Furniture* [1976]).

Qualifications to protection

As with unfair dismissal, qualification criteria exist that restrict the remedy only to an individual who:

- possesses 'employee' status;
- was continuously employed by the same employer for two years before the relevant date of the redundancy;
- is not in an excluded category of employee;
- was dismissed; and
- was dismissed on the basis of redundancy.

However, where suitable alternative employment/re-engagement with the employer or an associated employer is made, or where there is a 'relevant transfer' under **TUPE 2006**, there may be no dismissal. An employee who accepts the offer of alternative employment is entitled to a trial period of up to four weeks to ascertain if the work will be suitable. If the employee is dismissed from this position within the trial period, the dismissal will be held as being due to redundancy (**ERA 1996 s 138**).

Access to the right is also restricted to those individuals who were dismissed for misconduct or for involvement in industrial action.

Dismissal

The employee's claim can only be made if the tribunal finds they have been dismissed for the reason of redundancy. For a dismissal to be effective in a redundancy claim, the employee must have been given a specific date on which their employment will cease (termed as being put under notice of dismissal). The dismissal for the purposes of redundancy must be the actual notice of dismissal and not some future intention of the employer (*Morton Sundour Fabrics v Shaw* [1966]).

There is an exception to this rule whereby an employee may leave the employment before the redundancy becomes effective (**ERA 1996 s 142**). If the employee serves the employer with a 'counter-claim' within the statutory notice period of their intention to leave the employment early, and this is accepted by the employer, then the employee's right to claim a redundancy payment is protected.

In *Newcastle Upon Tyne NHS Foundation Trust v Haywood* [2018] it was held that notice of termination of employment is effective when received (in this case it was when the employee had returned from holiday)—even if this notice is sent via email.

The **ERA 1996 s 163(2)** assists the employee by presuming redundancy is the reason for the dismissal and placing the burden on the employer to disprove this.

Adopting a fair selection procedure

When the business is going to continue trading and some employees will be retained, the employer should ensure that a fair and transparent selection procedure of those chosen to be made redundant is applied.

Consultation requirements

When the employer is planning any collective redundancies involving 20 or more employees, there is an obligation to consult with the recognized trade union or other employee representatives (**TULRCA 1992 ss 188–198**). The appropriate employee representatives are identified in **TULRCA 1992 s 188(1B)**, although where an employer does not recognize a union, or has fewer than 10 employees, information and consultation may take place with the whole workforce.

The requirement is to begin the consultation process when the employer is 'contemplating' redundancies (*R v British Coal Corporation, ex p Vardy* [1993]).

TULRCA 1992 s 188(1A) provides that consultation must take place:

- where between 20 and 99 employees are to be made redundant, the minimum consultation period is a period of 30 days before the first dismissal;

- where over 100 employees are to be made redundant, the minimum period is 45 days before the first dismissal (see the **Trade Union and Labour Relations (Consolidation) Act 1992 (Amendment) Order 2013**).

✔ Looking for extra marks?

Critique the distinction between 'consultation' and 'negotiation' in relation to the requirements of the legislation and its application in the tribunal (see the Department of Trade and Industry's research report 'Redundancy Consultation: A Study of Current Practice and the Effects of the 1995 Regulations').

Calculation of the redundancy payment

The statutory remedy provided in the case of redundancy is compensation.

The payment is subject to a maximum figure (in the same way as unfair dismissal payments are subject to a maximum) and years in employment whilst under the age of 18 are not included in the calculation.

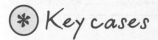 Looking for extra marks?

Note in your answer that the payment calculations are based on age discrimination, yet they continue to be permitted (see *MacMulloch v Imperial Chemical Industries Plc* [2008]).

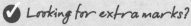 ⊛ Key cases

Case	Facts	Principle
Boston Deep Sea Fishing and Ice Co v Ansell (1888) LR 39 Ch D 339	Dismissal of a managing director for alleged dishonesty and later actual proof of the dishonesty is uncovered.	If an employer dismisses a worker, and later discovers evidence that proves that the worker was in fact guilty of alleged misconduct, this evidence will be accepted by the court and can justify a summary dismissal at common law as lawful.
British Home Stores v Burchell [1978] IRLR 379	Dismissal of an employee on suspicion of theft where there was a lack of firm evidence.	The principles established as to what would amount to reasonable suspicion required that the employer must: (1) honestly believe the employee is guilty; (2) have reasonable grounds on which to hold this belief; and (3) have carried out as much investigation into the matter as was reasonable in all the circumstances of the case.
Monie v Coral Racing Ltd [1980] IRLR 464	Dismissal of more than one employee on the basis of theft when an investigation could not identify who the perpetrator was.	The Court of Appeal held that to dismiss an employee on suspicion required solid and sensible grounds (not necessarily proof) on which to hold the belief.

Case	Facts	Principle
Western Excavating v Sharp [1978] IRLR 27	The case involved an employer's decision not to advance wages or provide a loan to an employee. The employee treated this refusal as a breach of the contract of employment and claimed constructive unfair dismissal.	There was no constructive dismissal. The employer had to breach a fundamental term of the contract to enable the employee to be successful. Further, the affected employee must choose to accept a repudiation within a reasonable time.
Williams v Compair Maxam [1982] IRLR 83	The case involved consultation with employees' representatives regarding redundancies.	Employers should seek to give as much warning of redundancies as possible to take remedial action, consult with the representatives regarding implementing the redundancies and applying the (objective) selection criteria, and the employer should consider employees being offered alternative employment.

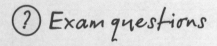
? Exam questions

Problem question

Helen is the manager of a bakery business that operates day and night shifts. Helen's job involves using the business computer to arrange the rotas, manage the staff pay, and update personnel data. She does not permit the staff to access the computer as the information held is strictly confidential, and as such it is password protected. All staff are informed that any unauthorized access of the computer will be treated as gross misconduct.

Abi, Claire, Jack, and Raavi are the employees working the night shift. When Helen arrives at work at 6am she discovers that during the night there has been unauthorized access of the computer, and confidential files and documents have been viewed. Abi, Claire, Jack, and Raavi are the only workers on duty during the night shift and therefore Helen considers that one or all of these members of staff must have been responsible. None of the staff had reason to access the computer.

Helen interviews each of the employees regarding their knowledge of the accessing of the computer, but each denies any involvement in the incident or knowledge of who may have been involved. She concludes that at least one of the employees is lying and so decides to dismiss Abi, Claire, and Jack immediately for misconduct. Helen decides not to dismiss Raavi as she believes he would not have been involved in the incident and three months ago he was promoted to a senior position due to his excellent work.

Following the dismissals, Helen continues her investigation and identifies that Jack was having an affair with a member of the administrative staff, Emma. Helen is convinced that Emma, who has access to the computer password, must have passed this on to Jack or another of the group, and dismisses her without notice. Emma was employed on a two-year fixed-term contract, of which she had served eight months.

Advise the parties of the rights and possible remedies in relation to this situation.

An outline answer is included at the end of the book.

Essay question

Identify the different remedies and protections for workers that are available through actions of unfair and wrongful dismissal. In your opinion, was statutory intervention, in the form of unfair dismissal, necessary to ensure workers had adequate remedies when dismissed? Justify your answer with reference to case law examples.

 Online Resources

To see an outline answer to this question log on to www.oup.com/lawrevision/

#9

Company law I: trading structures and forming the business

- It is important to recognize the distinct features between the five main forms of business organization (sole trader, simple partnership, limited liability partnership, private limited company, and public limited company).

- Sole trader organizations are very flexible but expose the owner to unlimited liability for losses, whilst operating a limited company limits potential losses of the shareholders but is subject to external regulation.

- There is no legal distinction between an individual trading as a sole trader and their business, but a limited company possesses its own legal personality irrespective of the members/directors who carry out its functions.

- A partnership can be 'simple', 'limited', or a 'limited liability partnership'.

- While partners generally have the right to participate in the management of the firm, shareholders of a limited company are not automatically allowed to take a part in its management.

- Private limited companies are not required to have a minimum share capital, but public limited companies require a minimum of £50,000 allotted share capital on registration.

Introduction

There exist significant implications for individuals and those with whom they trade on the basis of the type of business organization that is operated. Each of these provides advantages and disadvantages and there are implications for a business including taxation, succession, and regulation. Examination questions often focus on advising a person on which form of organization to adopt, and this involves a critique of the advantages and disadvantages of each.

Business organization

The five main types of business organization (trading structure) applicable in England and Wales are:

- Sole Trader;
- Simple Partnership;
- Limited Liability Partnership;
- Private Limited Company;
- Public Limited Company.

Sole traders

A sole trader is the simplest business organization due to the ease of establishing and dissolving the business. There is no formal registration process or mechanism to wind up the business (compare sole traders with limited companies/corporations). Key features of the sole trader are:

- the person carries on their business as an individual;
- they personally own the property and assets;
- they generally perform the work, unless they employ others or subcontract;
- they have unlimited liability for any acts or omissions of the business;
- they may have a business name, but this does not establish the business with a separate **legal personality** (as possessed by a limited company); and
- they must conform to the **Companies Act (CA) 2006 Part 41** (regarding the business name).

The sole trader has no responsibility to shareholders/partners and is merely responsible to themselves, their customers, and the State (such as registration with Her Majesty's Revenue and Customs (HMRC); registration for Value Added Tax (if applicable)). As such, there is relatively little additional external regulation of the business compared with corporations.

Of primary significance is that the sole trader has unlimited liability for the debts of the business. There is no difference between the assets of the business and those of the trader, with the result that any debts owed to creditors of the business can be claimed from the individual running the business.

Simple partnerships

A person may wish to form a business enterprise, and may seek to achieve this by forming a partnership with others. The **Partnership Act (PA) 1890 s 1** defines a simple partnership as the 'relation which subsists between persons carrying on a business in common with a view to profit'. This is of crucial importance in that whilst the Act states that the partner joins with a view to a profit, this does not mean that having not shared in any profits they do not qualify as partners (*M Young Legal Associates Ltd v Zahid* [2006]).

Establishing a simple partnership merely involves the partners agreeing to form the partnership (hence it need not be in writing and may be formed through verbal agreements or implied through conduct).

Types of partnership

There are three types of partnership. These are:

- An unlimited partnership (the most common type of partnership): the partners are responsible for the debts/liabilities of the firm (unlimited liability) and must satisfy these from their own assets if required.

- A limited partnership (under the **Limited Partnerships Act 1907**): requires that at least one of the partners agrees to accept full liability for any debts (while the other partners' loss is restricted to any capital/property invested (although this trading structure is not often used)).

- A firm can be established as a Limited Liability Partnership, to which the **Limited Liability Partnerships Act 2000** applies.

Types of partner

Generally there are four types of partner:

- A 'typical' partner is one who has the right to take part in the management of the firm (unless specifically agreed to the contrary).

- A 'silent'/dormant partner may come into the firm who invests money into the partnership but who does not take an active role in the management.

- A salaried partner does not have the rights and obligations of the other partners, and is essentially treated as an employee, but appears on the firm's letterhead.

- A partner by estoppel (a person who, through their words or conduct, either represents themselves as, or knowingly allows themselves to be represented as, a partner of the firm).

Partnership property

The **PA 1890 ss 20 and 21** identify that, in the absence of any agreement between the partners to the contrary, property will be considered partnership property where it has been purchased with partnership money, the partner who brought property into the firm has been credited with its value, or where it is treated as an essential part of the firm's property.

When the business is dissolved (having paid creditors), the partners will take back the property they brought to the firm.

Partners as agents

Partners are considered agents of the organization (**PA 1890 s 5**). This enables the partners to manage the organization, contract on behalf of the firm, and obligate the other partners as a result of this (lawful) action. This means that even if a partner does not have the actual authority to perform such actions, they may still bind the partnership under 'apparent' authority.

Revision tip

The agency rule in partnership is designed to protect the public who may not be aware of the internal power relations within the organization and trade with the partner in good faith.

Partners' liability

A crucial aspect of partnerships is of joint and several liability. This means that if one partner commits a tort/breaches a contract in the course of the business, the partnership will be liable (including each partner) if this was within the offending partner's actual or apparent authority (*Dubai Aluminium Co Ltd v Salaam* [2003]). If the partnership owes a debt to a creditor and there are insufficient resources of the organization to pay, then under the concept of unlimited liability, the partners have to satisfy the shortfall from their own resources. This liability will be shared equally between the partners based on their respective percentage ownership (joint liability). However, if one partner has resources and the other partner(s) does not have the resources to satisfy the debt, the partner with funds is responsible for the full debt (several liability—**PA 1890 s 9**). They then have the option to seek the money owed from the defaulting partner(s).

✔ *Looking for extra marks?*

When discussing joint and several liability, liability continues even when the partner has left the partnership for acts conducted whilst they were a partner. It is therefore important to be aware that there are several express and implied terms (obligations) on partners as to information they must disclose to other potential partners.

Partner duties

There exists in partnerships a fiduciary duty for the partners to act with loyalty to the partnership and in 'good faith':

- duty of disclosure: partners must submit full information to the other partners in matters affecting the organization and submit true accounts (**PA 1890 s 28**);
- duty to account: partners must account for any benefit they have obtained without consent from any transaction on behalf of the firm (**PA 1890 s 29**—see *Bentley v Craven* [1853]);
- duty not to enter into competition with the organization (**PA 1890 s 30**).

Rights of partners

Unless excluded by the partners, the **PA 1890** gives partners the following rights:

- the right to share equally in the capital and profits of the firm;
- the right to be indemnified by the firm for any liabilities or losses made in the normal course of business;
- the right to take a role in the management of the firm (but not for 'silent partners');
- an entitlement to inspect the partnership's accounts;
- the right to veto the entry of a new partner to the partnership or to change the partnership's business.

Limited liability partnerships

A simple partnership does not possess its own legal personality, and consequently the partners have unlimited liability for the debts of the firm. Conversely, a Limited Liability Partnership (LLP), established in accordance with the **Limited Liability Partnerships Act 2000**, possesses its own legal personality and its partners, to a large extent, enjoy limited liability.

The LLP must be registered with the Registrar of Companies (see section entitled 'Registrar of Companies').

The nature of an LLP possessing its own legal personality results in the following features (which are more akin to corporations than to partnership structures):

- Property of the LLP will belong to the business instead of belonging to the partners personally (as distinct from the situation in simple partnerships where the business does *not* possess its own legal personality and hence the property must belong to the individual(s) of the partnership).
- An LLP has perpetual succession (the partnership will continue despite changes to its internal membership and it will continue until formally wound up).

✅ *Looking for extra marks?*

The **Limited Liability Partnerships Act 2000 s 214A** has been beneficial to creditors of the LLP in that partners who have made withdrawals in the previous two years before the **winding-up** may be requested to return these sums if, during that period, the member knew, or ought reasonably to have known, that the LLP would become insolvent. **Section 74** ensures that members of the LLP and those members who have left, and who had established an agreement to contribute to the LLP upon dissolution, will contribute to the assets of the firm.

- The LLP is required to file its audited accounts and tax returns to the Registrar of Companies and the incorporation document must identify 'designated members' who will administer these and other matters on behalf of the LLP.

Revision tip

Typically, professional firms (firms of accountants, solicitors, etc) have taken the opportunity to become LLPs where the nature of their profession involves the risk of incurring trading debts. The exposure of the partners to risk, if the partnership could not settle any loss, is reduced.

Companies

The word 'companies' refers to corporations (incorporated businesses). The promoter (the person(s) who incorporate the company) registers the company in accordance with the legislative requirements and becomes the first shareholder, and in many cases the first director. The promoter is also responsible for the company's constitution. Companies may be private or public and may be limited or unlimited (although there are very few unlimited companies). (See Table 9.1.) The company must be registered in accordance with the CA 2006.

Registrar of Companies

Companies House is where the public can find information regarding companies and their directors, and the Registrar of Companies heads this office. The Registrar is responsible for:

- issuing of certificates of incorporation when a company is registered;
- maintaining records when a company's name is changed;
- maintaining records where the company is re-registered;
- listing the details of all registered companies, limited partnerships, and LLPs;
- maintaining the annual returns and accounts submitted by companies as required by law;
- maintaining the details of charges over company property;
- striking companies off the register when dissolved;
- maintaining the register of companies' special resolutions; and
- publishing details of the companies and the receipt of documents in the *London Gazette*.

Business organization

✳✳✳✳✳✳✳✳✳✳✳✳

Table 9.1 Distinctions between public and private companies

Private company	Public company
Its name must end with the word 'Ltd' or 'Limited'.	Its name must end with the words 'Public Limited Company' or 'PLC'.
A private company is prohibited from offering its shares to the public (**CA 2006 s 755**).	A PLC is entitled to offer its shares and debentures for sale to the public and it may be listed on, for example, the London Stock Exchange (although due to the Exchange's rules about which companies may be listed this is only applicable to the largest organizations).
A private company is not required to have a secretary (and if a private company chooses to have one, they do not have to be qualified).	A PLC requires a secretary and they must be qualified for the position.
There is no necessity to hold an Annual General Meeting (AGM).	The PLC must hold an AGM each calendar year.
No minimum share capital is prescribed.	The PLC must have an allotted share capital of £50,000 (one-quarter of the value of which must have been paid up).
Only one director is required.	At least two directors are required.
It can pass written resolutions.	It cannot pass written resolutions.

Limited companies

This is a very popular form of business enterprise and the changes introduced in the **CA 2006** continue with the process of removing many administrative procedures (especially in respect of private limited companies) that were required under the **Companies Act 1985**.

Companies may be registered as private limited or public limited and, following the **Company (Registration) Regulations 2008**, this designation is to appear in the 'Application for Registration' under the **CA 2006 s 9**.

Types of limited companies

- Limited by shares: this means that the amount due to the members of the company (the shareholders) if the company is wound up is limited to the nominal/par value of the shares they own.
- Limited by guarantee: this trading structure is generally used by not-for-profit organizations rather than 'businesses' and the 'guarantee' in this respect is a determined amount, established in the 'statement of guarantee' (see **CA 2006 ss 9(4) and 11**) which is to be paid when the company is wound up.

Legal personality

For a sole trader, there is no legal distinction between the person as an individual, and themselves operating the business (debts of the trader running the business may be claimed from their private assets). With limited companies (artificial legal things), upon incorporation the company itself possesses a separate legal personality distinct from the shareholders. Due to this legal personality, a company may enter into contracts on its own behalf, own property, etc. Separate legal personality is a key concept in company law.

Salomon v Salomon & Co Ltd [1897] AC 22

Salomon had been operating a sole trader business for many years, manufacturing boots. He later sold the business to a company which he formed. The company paid £39,000 for the business and Salomon left £10,000 of this figure in the company as his personal loan and established himself as a secured creditor (through a **debenture**). When the company failed, it only had assets of £6,000 which Salomon claimed as a secured creditor—leaving the remaining (unsecured) creditors with nothing. The House of Lords held that Salomon was entitled to the remaining money as the company had been correctly registered, and as a secured creditor he was entitled to the money before unsecured creditors.

Veil of incorporation

Separate legal personality distinguishes between the corporation as an entity and its shareholders. A 'veil' separates the company as an entity from the shareholders.

The metaphor identifies a cloak of secrecy/shield of the people behind the veil—the members of the company are protected from liability for the company's debts. However, the company must not be established to commit some fraud (*Jones v Lipman* [1962]) or to attempt to circumvent contractual agreements, otherwise the veil will be lifted to identify the true nature of the undertaking (*Gilford Motor Co Ltd v Horne* [1933]). *Adams v Cape Industries Plc* [1990] identifies circumstances when the veil will be lifted.

Features of a limited company

When determining the form of business organization to adopt, a corporation, being a separate entity from its members, provides advantages to those members and also empowers the company to take actions, accept liabilities, and so on that other business organizations may not. Therefore, some of its more important features will be identified in the following sections.

Limited liability

'Limited' in this respect refers to the potential liability of members of the company—the shareholders. The company itself has unlimited liability and therefore must satisfy any debts to creditors. The shareholders' liability for any debts is limited to the value they paid for the shares (which will likely become worthless if the company is wound up) or the money they owe on any shares (shares do not necessarily have to be fully paid for when they are issued).

> *Revision tip*
>
> This is a key element of limited companies. It enables investment in companies and enables entrepreneurs to take risks and expand the business into new areas without risk to their personal assets. Clearly, such a risk would limit the opportunity for innovation and expansion if the company's shareholders were personally financially responsible for any debts of the company. However, it imposes a risk for those trading with the limited company that they may not be able to seek money owed from those who ran or owned the business.

Perpetual succession

Once a company is established it remains in existence until it is legally wound up, regardless of who owns or runs the company. Therefore, when shareholders leave the company, a director dies/leaves the organization, and so on, this has no legal effect on the company's assets or ability to continue trading.

> *Revision tip*
>
> Note that perpetual succession enables businesses to benefit from investment of time and resources establishing a trustworthy image, reputation for a quality service/products, etc. This 'brand image' has a tangible benefit and may later be sold/used.

Single member companies

Both public and private companies may have only one member (shareholder). Remember, a director may not necessarily be a shareholder so this does not affect the requirement for public companies to have at least two directors.

Establishing the limited company

The three methods of establishing a limited company are:

- Royal Charter: examples include the British Broadcasting Corporation (BBC) and universities such as Oxford and Cambridge.
- Statute: examples include the utilities (before privatization) and bodies such as the Health and Safety Executive.
- Registration under the provisions of the CA 2006 (or under one of its predecessors, such as the Companies Act 1985). This is the most common and, in relation to the three forms available, the simplest way to form a company.

Registration procedure

Memorandum

The memorandum is a document available for public inspection and its aim is to identify the features of the company. It is not intended to form part of the company's constitution (as was previously the case) but, rather, to identify the company when it was formed (a 'snap-shot').

Articles of association

The articles are the constitution (rules) of the company and how it may run its affairs. This is the contractual agreement between the parties and the company, and may be established on the basis of a bespoke set of articles, or the company will use the default model articles established by regulations under the **CA 2006**.

The articles of a company may be later altered following registration through a special resolution (s **21**).

Section 22 allows for the entrenchment of articles to enable the amendment or repeal of specified provisions in the articles where conditions are met, or procedures are complied with that are more restrictive than those applicable in the case of a special resolution.

Certificate of incorporation

The company is established when the Registrar of Companies issues the certificate of incorporation. This document formally establishes the existence of the company and it will only 'die' when it is formally wound up.

The certificate provides the company with its legal status and personality that will enable it to trade and establish the contracts that enable the 'business' to begin.

Revision tip

If the promoters of the company make contracts supposedly on behalf of the company, but before the date when the company is incorporated, they will be held personally liable and they will not obtain protection from the limited liability status of the organization (**s 51(1)**).

Re-registration

A private company may choose to re-register as a PLC (or vice versa) and, once completed, a new certificate of incorporation is issued. The company will thereafter be subject to the rules applicable to its new status.

For a private company to re-register as a PLC, a special resolution must be passed under s **90** to enable a change in the articles to comply with the requirement to incorporate to a PLC.

A PLC may re-register as a private company through a special resolution. **CA 2006 s 97** requires that all of the company's members have assented to its being so re-registered. Due to the requirement for protection of the minority shareholders, s **98** provides that shareholders with a minimum of 5 per cent of the nominal value of the issued share

Business organization

****

capital, or if the company is not limited by shares by a minimum of 5 per cent of its members, or a minimum of 50 members, may apply to a court within 28 days of the resolution to have the special resolution terminated and made unenforceable as they were not in favour. It is for the court to determine whether the resolution should/should not be enforced.

Having identified each of the trading structures available when running a business, Table 9.2 offers an overview of their respective advantages and of their drawbacks.

Table 9.2 Advantages and disadvantages of the trading structure

Business organization	Advantages	Disadvantages
Sole trader	It is simple to establish.	The sole trader has unlimited liability.
	The sole trader is responsible to themselves and their customers.	Succession. The sole trader often trades under their own name. However, when the sole trader dies, their business may also die.
	The sole trader has autonomy in how they run the business, when they work, and how profits are disposed of (subject to HMRC rules).	They have complete responsibility for the business—to fulfil contracts, to invest money into the business, to employ replacements if they are ill or on holiday, and so on.
	They can begin trading immediately.	
Partnership	Partners often 'buy into' a partnership, therefore capital is frequently introduced.	Partnerships have unlimited liability and the partners' personal assets may be at risk for debts/losses.
	Partners may offer expertise in an area or provide the ability to enter into new markets.	Partners may create liabilities for the other partners and the firm.
	Partners may share the work of the business and share the liabilities.	Partners share in the profits of the firm therefore the individual partner's share may be reduced.
	Partnerships have several legal advantages, including ease of formation and dissolution, and they may provide tax advantages in certain circumstances.	Partners may be jointly and severally liable for losses.

Business organization	Advantages	Disadvantages
Limited Liability Partnership	The LLP has its own legal personality and limits the liability of its members.	It is subject to registration procedures with the Registrar of Companies.
	The partnership continues despite changes in the internal membership of the firm.	It must file accounts and tax returns to the Registrar.
		It has many features in common with limited companies; some of these are positive to the members and many have negative implications.
Limited companies	Limited liability for the members.	It has much greater administration requirements than other forms of business organizations.
	It has perpetual succession and only 'dies' when formally wound up.	It is subject to external and internal regulation.
	It is generally easier to raise finance than through a sole trader/partnership business organization.	There is no automatic right to participate in the management of the company.
	It can make contracts in its own right.	
	Tax benefits are available compared to other business organizations.	
	The company may offer fixed/floating charges over property.	
	Companies may be formed in the belief that the 'status' of a limited company provides an advantage over operating as a sole trader.	

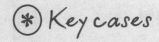 Key cases

Case	Facts	Principle
Salomon v Salomon & Co Ltd [1897] AC 22	Salomon operated a business as a sole trader until he sold it to the limited company he formed. He lent money to the company and registered himself as a secured creditor. When the company was wound up with debts, Salomon claimed the remaining money in the company in settlement.	The company had its own legal personality and the charges were correctly applied and registered. As such, Salomon was a secured creditor and ranked above unsecured creditors. These creditors were not able to challenge the status of the company (which had been correctly registered) even though it was in effect a 'one man' company.

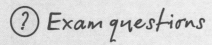 Exam questions

Problem question

Czarina wishes to reorganize her business. Czarina currently operates as a sole trader making and selling children's clothing from premises (which she rents) on the local high street. She wishes to expand her business to make clothes for department stores and this will probably require her to move to new premises and hire staff to assist her. Explain the options available to Czarina to reorganize her business, and outline the legal consequences of this.

An outline answer is included at the end of the book.

Essay question

The judgment in *Salomon v Salomon* [1897] should have been decided differently. It established that a correctly registered company possesses a legal identity separate from its shareholders. The result is a situation where unscrupulous traders may exploit a position of trust, and it has left unsecured creditors in a precarious position.

Using appropriate case law and practical examples, critically assess this statement. Justify your conclusions.

 Online Resources

To see an outline answer to this question log on to www.oup.com/lawrevision/

#10

Company law II: directors, finance, and capital

Key facts

- Directors exercise the specific tasks in the running of the company.

- The members (ie shareholders) 'own' the company but have no automatic rights of management.

- Directors may be appointed in accordance with the company's articles, usually through an ordinary resolution at a general meeting, but other mechanisms such as a written procedure may be valid.

- The common law duties on directors have been codified and expanded through the **Companies Act (CA) 2006**.

- Directors are responsible to the company itself, not to individual shareholders.

- Minority protection (of shareholders) is provided through the **CA 2006** to restrict directors' acts that may unfairly disadvantage them.

- Public companies must have a company secretary and they must satisfy statutory requirements in relation to their qualifications.

- A share is a bundle of rights and duties, and it imposes liabilities on the holder.

- Shareholders have no automatic right of management in the company although, through attendance and the rights to vote at shareholder meetings, they may have influence over the business conducted.

Introduction

The regulation of those who govern the company, and the protection of the shareholders, are particularly important aspects of company law. The roles played by directors, and the statutory duties imposed on them following enactment of the **CA 2006**, will increasingly form discrete examination questions, especially in relation to the codification of the common law principles upon which they are based.

Consideration must also be given to the broad issue of corporate governance, including rules on a company's opportunity to raise and maintain capital, and rules regarding the issuing of shares and granting of debentures, to protect the company and its creditors from abuse. In *Fons Hf v Corporal Ltd and another* [2014] the Court of Appeal defined the terms 'debenture' and 'securities' for the purposes of enforcing a share charge, having now determined that debenture includes a loan agreement.

Company directors

Executive directors are appointed to undertake the day-to-day tasks and decisions of the company (although other directors may be present in companies and who do not have these powers—eg non-executive directors).

Shareholders may, especially in larger companies, consist of a large and diverse population, therefore it would be impractical for each to have a management capacity and, hence, they appoint the directors to exercise the powers conferred on the position by the company.

Can a director be an employee?

Chapter 8 outlined the requirement that in order to qualify for protection against unfair dismissal, the individual must possess the employment status of employee. In *Stack v Ajar-Tec Ltd* [2015] the claimant, along with two other directors/shareholders, founded the company. Unlike a fellow founder of the company, Stack did not have a written contract of employment and whilst working for the company since its incorporation, he did not receive pay. Later, following difficulties in the relationship, Stack's directorship was terminated and he claimed an unfair dismissal payment. At the first tribunal hearing it was held that Stack was an employee. The tribunal considered that his promise to work for the company established an express agreement and it must be implied into this that he would be paid for this work. At appeal, the Employment Appeal Tribunal sent the case to a new tribunal to determine whether an employment contract could be implied on the basis of the facts. Stack appealed to the Court of Appeal which agreed that he was both an employee and a worker.

The case serves as a reminder for contractual formalities to be agreed from the outset and that directors, even where not paid, may be employees if the employer has an obligation to pay them.

Types of director

The **CA 2006 s 250** provides that '"director" includes any person occupying the position of director, by whatever name called'.

Directors of companies are often described with reference to their position and responsibilities to the company:

- executive director: so called due to their activities and because they undertake special responsibilities in the company—managing director, etc;

- non-executive director: has no duties over a specific area of the business and/or does not take an active part in the company's day-to-day management. Rather, they perform tasks such as attending meetings, taking part in the board's decision-making, etc;

- 'shadow director': defined as 'a person in accordance with whose directions the directors of the company are accustomed to act' (**CA 2006 s 251**).

Number of directors

- Private companies are required to have at least one director.

- Public companies must have at least two directors (**s 154**).

- The **Small Business, Enterprise and Employment Act 2015 s 87(2)** omits **CA 2006 s 155** with regards to the previous requirement that at least one director of the company be a natural (human) person. All new appointments of directors must be natural persons (**s 156A**). The appointment of new corporate directors is expected to be prohibited after October 2016 and existing corporate director appointments will automatically cease 12 months after this date—essentially giving companies a one year 'grace period' (**s 156C**). **Section 156B** allows the Secretary of State to make exceptions to this rule (such as pension trustee companies).

Appointment

The company's promoters are often the first directors of the company.

At some stage other appointments will occur, for example when existing directors leave or additional directors are required to add management expertise. The articles of association allow for the appointment of directors and authority for such action is usually through an ordinary resolution at a general meeting, although other mechanisms, such as a written procedure, may be equally valid. A **written resolution** is not an appropriate instrument for a director's removal.

A director must be at least 16 years of age when they undertake the directorship.

Revision tip

At a general meeting of a public company, a motion for the appointment of two or more directors by a single resolution must not be made unless a resolution that it should be so made has first been agreed (**s 160**). Any resolution that is passed in contravention of this section is void even if no one voted against the appointment of the directors.

Registration of directors

Every company is required to maintain a register of its directors and have it available for inspection (s 1136). The register must contain the information required under ss 163, 164, and 166 (the director's name, address, date of birth, etc).

A director's residential address is considered 'protected information' (s 240) and must not be disclosed except for the purposes of:

- communicating with the director; or

- sending information to the Registrar of Companies; or

- when compelled to do so following a court order.

✅ Looking for extra marks?

The **CA 2006** added protection to directors from having to disclose their residential address on these documents (as they are available for public inspection). This protection is in place to prevent abuse of, and possible attacks upon, directors, for example as seen in the case of directors of the company Huntingdon Life Sciences.

A potentially significant aspect of the **Small Business, Enterprise and Employment Act 2015** is for all UK companies (although not publicly listed companies) to maintain a register at Companies House of those persons who have significant control over the company (this is known as the PSC register). This may also apply to LLPs. Persons who possess the right to exercise significant influence or control—including controlling 25 per cent or more of the company's shares or voting rights, or control over the appointment/removal of the majority of the company's board of directors—would have to be included in this register. The company will have to establish and maintain this register, but will also require information from shareholders and others with relevant information to populate its contents.

Directors' duties

The CA 2006 codified and extended duties developed through the common law (see Table 10.1). The duties identified in ss 171–177 are owed by the director to the company (rather than those outside the company—*J J Harrison (Properties) Ltd v Harrison* [2001]).

Revision tip

CA 2006 s 170 provides that these general duties imposed on directors are to be interpreted and applied in the same way as the common law rules and equitable principles on which they were based.

To act within their powers

The director must act in accordance with the company's constitution (s 171) and only exercise powers for the purposes for which they had been conferred.

Table 10.1 Directors' duties

Directors' duties	CA 2006
To act within their powers	s 171
To promote the success of the company	s 172
To exercise independent judgement	s 173
To exercise reasonable care, skill, and diligence	s 174
To avoid conflicts of interest	s 175
Not to accept benefits from third parties	s 176
To declare an interest in proposed transactions or arrangements	s 177
Duty of the director to disclose interests in existing transactions/arrangements	s 182

Revision tip

Where authority is provided for a specific purpose, the power must only be used for this purpose and will not be extended (even if the director acted in good faith and for the best interests of the company—*Fraser v B N Furman (Productions) Ltd* [1967]).

To promote the success of the company

This was based on the common law duty of the director acting in good faith (s 172). The Act requires the director to fulfil this requirement in the way they consider would be most likely to promote the success of the company for the benefit of its members as a whole.

This requirement may instil an obligation of more strategic thinking on the part of directors who will consider the wider implications of their actions for the company's stakeholders, and consider the folly of short-term decision-making compared with taking a long-term view of the company's actions.

✅ *Looking for extra marks?*

The directors' duties articulated in s 172 generally involve the application of a subjective test—for example did the director know/should they have known about the likely insolvency and its effects on creditors? Where the director has failed to produce any evidence that they have given any consideration to these points, the test to be applied becomes an objective one. This situation is demonstrated in *Re HLC Environmental Projects Ltd, Hellard v De Brito Carvalho* [2013], which should be used and critiqued regarding the need for directors to demonstrate effective management, paper trails and evidence of decision-making, and continued vigilance of the company's affairs—especially when the company is in financial difficulties—to avoid breaching the duty.

Company directors
✳✳✳✳✳✳✳✳✳✳✳

To exercise independent judgement

The director has an obligation to exercise independent judgement (s 173) although this will not be infringed by their acting in accordance with an agreement entered into with the company or in a way authorized by the constitution of the company.

To exercise reasonable care, skill, and diligence

The duty is based on what a reasonably diligent person with the general knowledge, skills, and experience for carrying out the functions required of the director to the company would consider (an objective test). The duty is also based on the general knowledge, skill, and experience that the director actually possesses (a subjective test) (s 174).

To avoid conflicts of interest

A director has an obligation to avoid situations where they have, or can have, a direct or indirect interest that conflicts (or has the potential to conflict) with the interests of the company (s 175).

Not to accept benefits from third parties

A director of a company is not allowed to accept a benefit from a third party that is due to them being a director of the company and their acts or omissions as a director (s 176). The duty is not infringed where the acceptance of a benefit 'cannot reasonably be regarded as likely to give rise to a conflict of interest'.

To declare interest in proposed transaction or arrangement

If the director has, directly or indirectly, an interest in a proposed transaction or arrangement with the company, this interest must be declared to the other directors with specific regard to the nature and extent of the interest (s 177). The declaration may be made in the following way, although others may be used:

* at a meeting of the directors; or
* by notice to the directors in accordance with s 184 (notice in writing) or s 185 (general notice).

Duty of the director to disclose interests in existing transaction/arrangement

Beyond the codification of the common law duties imposed on directors, the CA 2006 imposes duties on the director who has an interest (direct or indirect) in a contract or proposed contract with the company to disclose this as soon as is reasonably practicable (s 182). This duty is somewhat different from those listed in ss 171–177 as it imposes a criminal, rather than civil, liability (but note that disclosure under s 177 can obviate the need for disclosure under s 182).

Transactions requiring member approval

The following transactions between a director and the company must be approved by the members:

- where a director's contract of employment is for a term in excess of two years (s 188);
- loans to a director;
- substantial property transactions; and
- awards of sums in excess of £200 on loss of office.

Civil consequences of a breach of the duties

Where there is a breach (or threatened breach) of the duties identified in ss 171–177, the consequences are the same as provided in the common law rules or equitable principles (s 178).

Where the director has transgressed the requirements under this part of the Act, they may be liable to compensate the company for any losses sustained due to the breach.

Revision tip

It must also be remembered that even beyond the responsibilities of the director to the company and any imposition of responsibility through the **CA 2006**, a director who disregards these duties may suffer a disqualification if they appear unfit to fulfil the role of director (**Company Directors Disqualification Act 1986**).

In *Cullen Investments Limited and others v Brown and others* [2017], the High Court heard the case of brothers who breached their duties as directors by diverting a commercial opportunity for their own benefit (which should have been made to the company). Whilst it is open for the courts to relieve directors from their liability if they had acted honestly and reasonably, this was not the case here. The test of honesty is subjective (did the director believe their conduct would not breach their duties)? Reasonableness is an objective test—did the director meet the standards expected of a competent director?

Directors' powers

The authority of the directors to take decisions will be identified in the articles of association. The authority refers to the directors' powers of management, but the directors must act within their powers. An act beyond these powers may later be ratified by the members of the company through an ordinary resolution (or special resolution if the act was outside the company's objects—what are now the company's articles).

Removal of a director

Directors may leave/be removed from office for numerous reasons including:

- their death in office;
- they may resign (which the company is obliged to accept);
- upon dissolution of the company, the directors are automatically dismissed;
- they may retire;
- they may be disqualified from holding office;
- the shareholders/board may wish to remove the director before their term of office has expired.

A director may be removed from office through an ordinary resolution (s 168). Special notice is to be provided of 28 days to the company secretary of the resolution and the meeting at which the resolution is to be passed must be called with at least 21 days' notice.

Where a director is also a shareholder, they are entitled, of course, to cast their votes against removal from office. And sometimes a company's constitution may give a shareholder who is also a director, and is threatened with removal from office, extra or 'weighted' votes. The legality of such clauses was upheld in the following case.

Bushell v Faith [1970] AC 1099

A company had 300 shares split equally between three shareholders, who were a brother and his two sisters (the directors were the brother and one of the sisters). The sisters wished to remove the brother as director and proposed a resolution to this effect; however, the articles provided that where a director was to be removed from office, in the vote to move this resolution, the affected director's shares should carry three votes per share. As such, following the vote, the two sisters' shares accounted for 200 votes, whilst the brother's 100 shares accounted for 300 votes, and the vote to remove the director was defeated.

A director who is subject to a resolution to have them removed from office may protest. The CA 2006 provides the director with the right to be heard on the resolution at the meeting through a written representation to the company members (not exceeding a reasonable length) unless this would be an abuse of the rights provided in s 169.

Beyond the use of the CA 2006 for this removal, there may be provision in the company's articles to achieve the same result. For example, the company may incorporate a clause into the articles that the director could be removed with a majority vote by the board by notice in writing. The main use of a removal through the articles rather than through s 168 is simply that in the case of subsidiary companies, a holding company is not entitled to use s 168 to remove directors of the subsidiary, but through the articles this is achievable.

A director may not be removed from office through s 168(1) by means of a written resolution.

Disqualification of directors

The legislation used to prevent a director holding office is the **Company Directors Disqualification Act 1986** and it may be applied to both natural persons and to corporations that hold directorships.

Examples of the offences that may lead to disqualification include:

* Conviction of an indictable offence in connection with the promotion, formation, management, or liquidation of a company, or with the management or receivership of the company's property (s 2).

* Where the director has been persistently in default in providing the required annual returns or accounts to the Registrar (s 3). From 2016, the annual return was replaced with an annual 'confirmation statement'. This confirmation statement is intended to remove 'red tape' and provide a simplified system whereby companies will simply check and confirm that information required to be filed at Companies House is maintained.

* If an officer or receiver of a company in liquidation has been guilty of fraud in relation to the company, or has breached their directors' duties, or committed an offence of knowingly being a party to fraudulent trading (s 4).

* If the person acting as a director (or shadow director) had been engaged in conduct that led to a company becoming insolvent and it is considered that they are unfit to act in a management capacity (s 6).

* If the person is an undischarged bankrupt (s 11).

* A court may make a disqualification order against a person if they have been instructing an unfit director of an insolvent company (**Small Business, Enterprise and Employment Act 2015 s 105**).

* The **Small Business, Enterprise and Employment Act 2015 s 104** provides that certain convictions abroad (a relevant foreign offence) may lead to a director's disqualification.

Revision tip

The action that leads to a person being disqualified for unfitness is not restricted to actions taken in the UK—its jurisdiction is much broader (*Re Seagull Manufacturing Co (No 2)* [1994]).

Where a person ignores the order, they commit a criminal offence and can be held personally liable for any debts/liabilities incurred whilst acting in the capacity.

✔ *Looking for extra marks?*

In an essay question regarding disqualification, you may wish to critique the purpose of the Act—not to punish the director but instead to protect the public from the activities of unfit persons to be concerned with company management. Consider the deterrent effect of this underlying purpose, especially in light of *Secretary of State for Trade and Industry v Tjolle and Others* [1998].

Directors' liability to shareholders

The directors of a company and the company secretary owe duties to the company as a whole rather than to the individual shareholders (who make up the company) and as such the shareholders are unlikely to be able to claim directly against the director based on their conduct (although exceptions exist).

Minority protection

Shareholders have the right, and the company is obliged in certain circumstances, to place a resolution at a general meeting and have this voted upon by the members (the shareholders). Shareholders holding fewer than 50 per cent of the voting shares may be outvoted, in ordinary resolutions, by the majority. As such, they are vulnerable to potential abuse.

Directors may be shareholders and they may form a majority and, hence, would find it relatively easy to pass through the resolutions that require a simple majority, or even those requiring a 75 per cent majority (special resolutions).

Foss v Harbottle [1843] 2 Hare 461

Two directors sold part of their own land to the company and a claim was made by the minority shareholders (on the company's behalf) that the price paid by the company was too high. The court refused to hear the action. It held that the interest in the case belonged to the company, and if the company believed the directors had acted wrongfully, then it should determine whether to bring the action against the directors—not the minority shareholders.

As identified in *Foss*, shareholders, in specific circumstances, may bring a claim on behalf of the company against its directors—known as a derivative claim. Whilst *Foss* did not assist shareholders' protection, statutory protection is provided in s 260.

The **CA 2006** has introduced protections for minority shareholders where a shareholder may initiate proceedings against a director on the company's behalf (a derivative claim). The proceeding will be in respect of a cause of action arising from an actual or proposed act or omission by a director of the company. Such acts or omissions could involve negligence, default, breach of duty, or breach of trust.

However, as this is a claim through the shareholders on the company's behalf, any award will be provided to the company. The shareholder claimant may be able to recover any expenses incurred in the action.

To pursue a derivative claim, the member must obtain the court's permission to proceed with their action (s 261):

- the first stage is to determine whether a prima facie case exists against the director; and, where satisfied,

- the court may give directions as to the evidence to be provided by the company, it may give permission for the claim to continue on the terms it sees fit, refuse permission and dismiss the claim, or adjourn proceedings and give any directions it thinks fit.

Another area of protection available to the minority shareholder, rather than a derivative claim, is where their rights have been 'unfairly prejudiced' by the way in which the company is being run.

Unfair prejudice

The protection of members against unfair prejudice is contained in the **CA 2006 Part 30**. It provides a right for members to petition a court that the company's affairs are being conducted in a manner that is likely to unfairly prejudice the interests of members generally, or some part of its members (including at least themselves). The member may also petition on the basis that an actual or proposed act or omission of the company is or would be so prejudicial (**s 994**).

The **CA 2006** also provides a right for the Secretary of State to exercise powers to petition the court where they believe the rights of members are being unfairly prejudiced (s **995**).

Where the court is satisfied that the petition is well founded, it has a general discretion to offer any relief it thinks necessary, with the specific forms of relief noted in s **996** being examples. The court is empowered in s **996(2)** specifically:

- to order as it thinks fit relief in respect of the matters complained of;
- to require the company to refrain from doing or continuing an act complained of (**subs (2)(b)(i)**);
- to do an act that the petitioner has complained it has omitted to do (**subs (2)(b)(ii)**);
- to authorize civil proceedings to be brought in the name of (and on behalf of) the company by such person(s) and on such terms as the court may direct (**subs (2)(c)**);
- to provide for the purchase of shares of any members of the company by other members (or by the company itself) (**subs (2)(e)**).

Re Bankside Hotels Ltd, Re Pedersen (Thameside) Ltd, Re G&G Properties Ltd [2018] confirms that whilst relief from a claim of unfairly prejudicial behaviour is available at the court's discretion, it is still required to satisfy itself that such behaviour has occurred. This applies, as in *Bankside*, where the allegation is no longer contested.

To regulate the conduct of the company's affairs in the future, the court may order the altering of its articles to prevent future abuses. Note that where this has occurred any future attempt to alter the articles through a special resolution will require the court's permission.

Examples of activities that may unfairly prejudice minority shareholders include:

- directors being negligent in their management of the company;
- directors paying themselves salaries that reduce or remove entirely the members' dividends (*Re Sam Weller & Sons Ltd* [1989]);

- issuing shares to directors on much more favourable terms than available to members;

- a shareholder is refused a management role with the company where there was an understanding between the shareholders and that excluded shareholder that they would be entitled to participate in management (*Re London School of Electronics* [1985]).

Revision tip

Where a director (and shareholder) of a company has been removed and therefore can no longer take an active part in its management, the court has often ruled that the majority shareholders must purchase the shares of the removed director.

✅ *Looking for extra marks?*

Note that in relation to unfair prejudice, the rulings in the cases given do not prevent a petition for the winding-up of the company on just and equitable grounds (*Re Company (No 001363 of 1988)* [1989]).

Company secretary

The **CA 2006** removed the requirement for private (but not public) companies to have a secretary. The secretary carries out administrative duties on the company's behalf.

Although a private company is not required to have a secretary (s 270), the powers and duties attributable to a director and a secretary cannot be performed by one person (a sole director).

Consequently, whilst the company may legally have just one member, it is required to have at least two officers—director and secretary. The secretary is also considered to be an employee of the company and this must be taken into account with regard to the rights of employees and the duties on employers, and also if the company is wound up.

Shares

A share is a bundle of rights and duties that the holder possesses in relation to the company and the other members. 'Rights' in this respect includes attendance at meetings, powers to vote, or an entitlement to a dividend, etc.

Shares also impose liabilities on the owner to contribute the amount of capital required to be paid when called-up by the company (eg if the shares had not been fully paid for).

Features of the share are:

- the share must have a fixed nominal value or it is void (s 541); and

- each share must be distinguished by its appropriate number except when the shares are fully paid up and rank without preference (***pari passu***), or all the issued shares of a particular class are fully paid up and rank *pari passu* for all purposes (s 543).

Share capital

When the company limited by shares is formed, the subscribers (original shareholders of the company) identify the amount of capital they have received from the share issue. The identification of the share capital reassures the company's creditors that sufficient funds (capital) are present in the event that the business fails and that the company will be in a position to satisfy its debts. It is for this reason that there are detailed provisions concerning how a company may alter or reduce its share capital.

Shares are required to have a nominal value (s 542). This nominal value is the amount that the company and the purchaser have agreed as the purchase price for the share (unless allotted at a premium) and this value may not be lowered (or this would constitute a fraud on the company).

Note that the nominal value is the lowest price that the share will be sold for but it may be possible (and indeed could prove advantageous) for the share to be transferred at a higher value than this, and this value is the share premium.

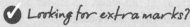

Looking for extra marks?

Where a company manages to receive a premium on the shares issued, this must be transferred into a share premium account (s 610). It must not be distributed to the members as dividends or be used to write off expenses such as when debentures are issued or for any costs incurred in forming the company.

Shares are usually issued to raise capital whereas loans taken by the company (generally secured on the company's assets) have to be repaid in accordance with the loan agreement.

- a private limited company is not required to have any prescribed amount of share capital;
- a public limited company's requirement is £50,000.

Dividend payments

Dividends may only be paid from the company's distributable profits (and in cash unless otherwise stated in the articles) as to do otherwise would be to reduce the company's capital.

Loan capital

At some stage a company may have to borrow money to buy stock, invest in technology or premises, and so on.

In order to obtain a loan, the lender will require some security (collateral). This security will be in the form of:

- a fixed charge (a charge applied to a specific property—such as factory premises);
- a floating charge (a charge over a group of assets—such as stock).

Fixed charges

The benefit of the fixed charge for the lender, and a reason why they may pursue such a charge in determining whether to loan money, is the control over the property. It therefore represents the best form of security.

The borrower may be prevented from selling the property that is subject to the charge until the loan is repaid, and the charge remains until the loan is fully repaid. Further, a lender with a fixed charge ranks above preferential creditors and creditors who possess floating charges.

Floating charges

As opposed to a charge that is fixed to a particular asset, the borrower may apply the charge to a group of existing and future assets (eg the stock with which the company trades).

The benefit for the borrower in this scenario is that they are free to trade in the goods/assets subject to the floating charge and, in the event of non-payment of the loan when it is due, the charge becomes fixed or 'crystallizes' over them. At this stage, the lender has the ability to dispose of the goods in the same way as someone with a fixed charge.

Crystallization occurs where:

- a receiver is appointed;
- if the company goes into administration or is wound up; or
- where an event that was provided for in the contract establishing the floating charge occurs.

If the borrower were to trade in the assets after crystallization occurs, the holder of the charge may bring an action against them.

To prevent fraud, and perhaps a situation of the borrower attempting to obtain multiple loans on the assets subject to a charge, protection is afforded through a system of registration.

Registration of charges

The register is a public document which interested parties may consult before deciding to do business with a company. The company is required to maintain its own copy of the register of charges at its registered office or other suitable place, and this must be made freely available for inspection by the company's creditors or members (s 877).

> *Revision tip*
>
> If the company does not register the charge in its register the officers of the company are liable to be fined (s 876(4)).

Within 21 days of the creation of a charge it is required to be registered (note, however, that some charges are not registered). It is also possible for a person interested in the registration to register it. The Registrar will then issue a certificate of registration and include details as to its particulars (s 869). The right of the 'person interested' to be able to register the charge exists because where a charge is not registered, it will be invalid and it will not allow the creditor to have the right to dispose of the assets to which the charge was to relate. This does not mean that the creditor would be unable to bring an action against the company on the debt owed, but they would lose the security that the charge provides (an unsecured creditor).

Priority of charges

If the charges have been correctly registered, they rank in priority as follows:

- Fixed charges rank higher than existing floating charges unless the existing floating charge has made provision against this (fixed charges have effect from the time they are created).

- Preferential creditors take priority over the holders of floating charges, but not over fixed charges. Preferential creditors include employees.

- Floating charges (takes effect when it crystallizes) have priority according to when the charge was created (hence the first floating charge will have priority over the last one created over the same asset, unless the contrary is stated).

Revision tip

Payments to the government are no longer included in the list of preferential creditors (**Enterprise Act 2002**).

Preferential creditors

Preferential creditors are entitled to payment for the following debts:

- unpaid wages (to a maximum of £800);
- unpaid holiday pay;
- contributions to occupational pension schemes; and
- loans taken to pay wages/holiday pay.

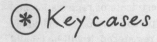 **Key cases**

Case	Facts	Principle
Bushell v Faith [1970] AC 1099	A director of a family-owned company was subject to a resolution to remove him before the expiration of his term of office. He was also a shareholder and the articles provided that the shares held by a director, who was to be removed in such a way, would carry three votes per share. As he and his two sisters were the shareholders with 100 shares each, he defeated the resolution 300 votes to 200.	The use of an ordinary resolution to remove a director may prove problematic where they are also a shareholder and the articles provide for specific protection against removal from office.
Foss v Harbottle [1843] 2 Hare 461	Minority shareholders attempted to bring a claim on the company's behalf. They considered the directors had sold their own land to the company for an inflated price.	Minority shareholders could not bring a claim—it was for the company to bring a claim if wrongdoing was alleged, not the minority shareholders. This 'derivative claim' procedure has been given greater protection through statutory intervention.
Panorama Developments (Guildford) Ltd v Fidelis Furnishing Fabrics Ltd [1971] 3 All ER 16	A company secretary hired cars on the company's behalf but used these for his own purposes.	Third parties are protected when contracting with a company agent (such as its secretary). The secretary generally has authority to agree contracts connected with the administration of the company, and this led to the company having to pay the bill for the car hire. (This would not remove the secretary's liability to the company though.)

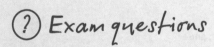 **Exam questions**

Problem question

Advanced Electronics Ltd (AEL) is a private company with three directors (one of whom is the managing director). The directors of the firm are subject to the duties that have been imposed following the enactment of the Companies Act 2006. These directors require an understanding of the effects that this legislation has placed on them beyond the common law duties previously regulating their actions. Specifically, one of the directors—Jubril—has signed a contract for AEL to sell laptop computers manufactured by Orange Computers Inc following an all-expenses-paid sales conference for one week at a five-star golf and leisure resort in Spain. While the laptops made by Orange Computers

Inc are very good, the profit margin on them is low compared to similar laptops that can easily be sourced elsewhere.

Prepare an outline of the effects of the Companies Act 2006 on directors' duties generally, and the specific action that the company should take to ensure compliance with the legislation in relation to Jubril.

An outline answer is included at the end of the book.

Essay question

Explain the authority that the company secretary possesses to bind the company, and how the concept of apparent authority may protect third parties who contract on this basis.

To see an outline answer to this question log on to www.oup.com/lawrevision/

#11

Intellectual property and data protection

Key facts

- The law of copyright is governed by the **Copyright, Designs and Patents Act (CDPA) 1988** that protects original materials including literary, dramatic, musical, artistic works, and typographical arrangements.

- Design rights protect the appearance/shapes of a product (such as the Coca-Cola bottle) and the design must be fixed and original (not commonplace).

- Unregistered design rights exist for a shorter period than registered designs and the owner has to demonstrate that the transgressor deliberately copied the design (which can be difficult).

- The **Trade Marks Act 1994** protects the owner of any sign capable of being represented graphically and which is capable of distinguishing the goods or services of one undertaking from those of another.

- Registration of a patent prevents others from making, using, or selling the same product without permission. The protection lasts for five-year periods (to a maximum of 20 years).

- From 1 October 2014 the **Intellectual Property Act 2014 (IPA)** commenced, which alters aspects of intellectual property (IP) law such as design law by introducing criminal liability for infringement. The European Union (EU) has also attempted to make protection and enforcement of IP easier through a proposed Unitary Patent and Unified Patent Court.

- From 2018 businesses have obligations to protect the data of individuals. The **General Data Protection Regulation** and the **Data Protection Act 2018** regulate activities in this area.

Introduction

The protection of IP rights is significant for businesses which may have spent considerable sums in developing copyrighted materials, patents, and trade marks (see Fig 11.1). Unauthorized use of these materials, deliberately or innocently, may breach the owner's IP rights, and enforcement proceedings may be the result. IP is often a very valuable commercial asset that can be exclusively used by the owner, sold, and licensed. It may provide a significant revenue stream for businesses.

As an overview of the interrelationship between forms of IP, the UK Intellectual Property Office (UK-IPO) provides an example of the applicability of IP in terms of a mobile telephone:

- the ringtone would be covered through copyright;
- its shape is protected through a registered design;
- the name of the phone or associated logo could be protected through a registered trade mark; and
- the processes used in its manufacture can be protected through patents.

✅ Looking for extra marks?

Awareness of the interaction between different IP rights, and demonstrating their overlap in many cases, will show an examiner your complete understanding of the topic.

Figure 11.1 Forms of Intellectual Property

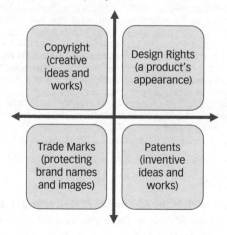

Copyright

Copyright exists to prevent others from taking unfair advantage of the creativity of a person. However, the prevention only exists for defined periods (see Table 11.1). The law is governed, through statute, by the **CDPA 1988** (as amended by the **Copyright and Related Rights Regulations 2003**) and through the **EU Copyright Directive 2001/29/EC**. The **CDPA 1988** provides rights to person(s) who may lawfully use the work and identifies how permission to use the work will be granted (eg through licensing).

Under the Copyright Directive 2001/29/EC, 'work' requires, 1) that the subject matter concerned is an original intellectual creation; and 2) there must be an 'expression' of that original intellectual creation.

Revision tip

Copyright need not be applied for, and actions for the unauthorized use of the owner's copyright may proceed once the work has been fixed (eg being recorded and written down). For example, you may hear a musician devise a tune on a harmonica whilst being interviewed (think Bruce Springsteen here) but copyright of the tune will only take effect if it is recorded.

Copyright protection may be granted to expressions, but not to ideas, procedures, methods of operation, or mathematical concepts.

Case C-310/17 Levola Hengelo BV v Smilde Foods BV **[2018] ECLI:EU:C:2018:899**

The Court of Justice of the European Union (CJEU) heard a case from a Dutch court regarding the copyright protection of food. A spreadable dip with cream cheese called 'Heksenkaas', created in 2007 by a Dutch retailer, had been transferred to a different company, Levola. In 2014 another company manufactured and sold, through a supermarket chain, a similar product. Levola argued that this product infringed its copyright (under the **Copyright Directive 2001/29/EC**) as to the taste of 'Heksenkaas'. The CJEU confirmed that to be protected under copyright the taste of a food product must be capable of being classified as a 'work' within the meaning of the Directive. This required the subject matter concerned to be an original intellectual creation, and it must be an 'expression' of that original intellectual creation. These criteria could not be met and therefore the ruling established that the taste of a food product cannot be classified as 'work' and gain protection under the Directive.

Ownership

Generally, the author of a work is the first owner of the copyright. Where an employee has created the work in the course of their employment, then unless agreed to the contrary, the employer is the first owner (s 11(1) and (2)).

Protection

The copyright holder is entitled to protection where the work fulfils the following criteria:

- the work is of a type that is protected in the **CDPA 1988**;
- it has been produced in some tangible form—written, recorded, and so on;
- the work satisfies the requirement of originality; and
- the owner/creator is a British citizen and/or the work was first published in the UK (**ss 154 and 155**).

Note that following the commencement of the **Berne Convention for the Protection of Literary and Artistic Works** (to which the UK is a party), 'foreign' authors are given the same rights and protections in relation to copyrighted materials as are domestic authors in those signatory countries.

Revision Tip

The term 'original' does not refer to an idea or thought that is original but, rather, it is the expression of the idea that must be original (it originated from the creator and was not copied from another's work).

The copyright standards are therefore quite low, but protection is afforded to prevent continuous copyrighting of works through modification of an original.

Copyright allows the owner to protect breaches of the unauthorized use of *original* and qualifying material which include (s 1(1)):

- *literary works* (s 3): including books, computer software programs, song lyrics, etc;
- *music and broadcasts* (ss 5 and 6): including films, videos, and radio shows;
- *dramatic productions*: including plays and dances;
- *artistic works* (s 4): this is wide ranging and includes drawings, diagrams, logos, photographs, etc;
- *typological arrangements of published editions* (s 8): this involves the planning and establishing of type that may then be printed. Examples include sections of a newspaper and the layout of a book.

Revision Tip

It is not possible to claim copyright protection for ideas; or names, phrases, and slogans (although they may be applicable to trade mark protection); or products and manufacturing processes (although patents may be applicable).

Copyright

✳✳✳✳✳✳✳✳✳✳✳✳

Legal rights

The owner's legal rights allow them to (**s 16**):

- copy and distribute copies of the work to the public;
- perform, show, or play the work in public (eg through various broadcast media);
- broadcast the work/communicate it to the public;
- make an adaptation of the work or do any of the above in relation to an adaptation;
- under the **Artist's Resale Rights Regulations 2006**, an artist has the right (resale right) to a percentage of the selling price (resale royalty) when they own the copyright and certain forms of art are sold.

Moral rights

The owner has the legal rights to the work, but it must be recognized that the author holds moral rights (beyond those economic rights—**s 77**). These rights include:

- protection against the distortion of the owner's work;
- in relation to literary, dramatic, artistic, or musical works, they have the right to be recognized as the author of the work whenever it is performed commercially or in public;
- literary, dramatic, artistic, or musical works may not be falsely attributed to an author;
- where an undertaking has been made to make a film or take photographs for private consumption, they may not show or broadcast this to the public.

Remember: the **IPA 2014** allows for the reasonable copying of sound recordings, films, and broadcasts which are used for non-commercial research and private study, without the need for obtaining the permission of the copyright holder.

Duration of protection

Table 11.1 Duration of protection of copyright

Type of original works	Duration of copyright
Sound recordings	50 years
Broadcasts	50 years
Literary and dramatic works	The life of the creator plus 70 years
Typographical arrangements	25 years
Publication of a literary, dramatic, musical, or artistic work (previously unpublished) and commercially exploited	25 years
Databases	15 years

Infringement of copyright

Primary and secondary infringement

Infringement of copyright exists where a qualitatively substantial part (not necessarily the whole) of the work is copied (s 16(3)(a) and (b)).

> ### Revision tip
>
> The term 'substantial' is determined by the quality of what has been copied rather than an assessment of the quantity. It may be necessary, therefore, to consider the copied work in isolation to the remainder of the defendant's work.

Primary infringement of copyright occurs when one or more of the exclusive 'legal' rights of the owner has been breached (s 16(2))—hence performed/used without the permission of the owner (knowledge of the infringement is not required).

Breach of a secondary infringement (s 22) requires that the perpetrator knows, or should have known, of the existence of the copyright of the work being infringed. Further, this is for some reason other than for the person's own personal/domestic use (hence, to exploit this infringement commercially), and the person does not have the owner's permission (licence). Secondary infringement occurs where the person, without the owner's permission:

- imports an article into the UK;
- possesses an article in the course of business;
- sells/lets for hire or offers for sale/hire such an article;
- in the course of business exhibits in public or distributes an article; or
- otherwise than in the course of business distributes to an extent that it prejudicially affects the owner of the copyright of an article.

Exceptions to infringement of copyright

The following is a non-exhaustive list. The IPA 2014 provides for situations where the lawful use of another person's copyrighted material is possible in the absence of the owner's permission:

- Non-commercial research and private study: allows a non-owner of copyright to copy limited extracts of works when this is used for non-commercial research or private study and the amount of materials taken was reasonable and appropriate for those purposes (what is known as fair dealing).
- Criticism and review: the fair dealing exception to copyright material extends to where the works have been used for criticism, review, or quotation (with the exception of a photograph).

Copyright
****

- People with disabilities: two exceptions exist to copyright where these offer a benefit to disabled people (which may be a physical or mental impairment). First, a copy of lawfully obtained copyright material in a format that helps the individual with the disability to access it may be produced. Secondly, educational establishments and charities may make accessible copyrighted materials on the behalf of persons with disabilities. These exceptions will only apply where the newly formed accessible materials have not been available commercially.

- Time-shifting: given the changes to digital services and the way that individuals consume media, time-shifting enables individuals to record a broadcast which is intended for private and domestic use and can be viewed or listened to at a time convenient for that purpose.

- Personal copy: individuals may copy such media, which they own, for the purpose of backing up (and for personal use).

- Parody: some copyrighted materials may be used by individuals without the owner's permission for the purposes of parody, caricature, or pastiche. This is based on fair dealing.

Remedies

The following remedies are available for infringement:

- damages;
- injunction;
- delivery of the product;
- account of profits.

Criminal offences

Criminal offences (identified in s 107) may be committed by a person who:

- offers for sale or hire;
- imports into the UK otherwise than for their own private and domestic use; or
- possesses, in the course of business, with a view to committing an act infringing copyright,

an article which is, or they have reason to believe is, infringing copyright of a work. The defendant may, if found guilty, be liable, on summary conviction, to imprisonment for a period not exceeding six months.

Defences/permitted acts

- Public interest disclosure (*Hyde Park Residence Ltd v Yelland* [2000]—regarding the use of security footage of Princess Diana and Dodi Al-Fayed by the *Sun* newspaper);
- Where the user is granted limited use of the material for non-commercial research or study (eg copying a section of a book);

- Where the materials are used for reporting events/court proceedings; and
- If the materials are used in reviews.

Design rights

Design rights may be seen in the development of a product's shape and design that make its appearance stand out (eg the Coca-Cola bottle). Design rights are applicable to three-dimensional works only, but the unregistered community designs procedure (under EU law) does protect two-dimensional products.

A design right is established, and the period of protection begins, when the work is first 'fixed' in design documents such as a drawing or when it is first made. The design must be an original, and in demonstrating that it is not commonplace, the owner should maintain their records of the design's development (eg in email communications, plans, and files).

Various forms of design right exist, as shown in Table 11.2. The copyright protection is effective where the design is artistic or involves plans and drawings, and the design is not intended to be mass-produced.

Further protection, not only of preventing the design being copied without permission but also of controlling the exploitation of the design in any manufacturing of products, is available upon registration under the **Registered Designs Act (RDA) 1949** (protection exists for a period of 25 years).

Revision tip

It is important to recognize that in the final five years of the design right's period of protection, its owner is obliged to agree licensing terms with third parties who wish to use the design. Where no agreement can be reached, the terms are decided by the UK-IPO.

Table 11.2 Duration of protection of design right

Design right	Duration of protection
UK registered design	Five years from the date of filing (renewable in five-year periods to maximum of 25 years).
UK unregistered design	Automatic—ten years from the first marketing of the product or 15 years after the design's creation (whichever is earlier).
EU registered design	Five years from the date of filing (renewable in five-year periods to maximum of 25 years).
EU unregistered design	Five years from the date the design was first made available to the public.

Registered designs

Whilst the design right provides protection without any form of registration, it must satisfy the requirements of originality of the design. This right is governed by the **CDPA 1988 Part III** and may be considered closely related to copyright.

However, greater protection is afforded the owner if they register at the Patent Office (Designs Registry) under the **RDA 1949** (which is more closely related to patents). In the case where damages are sought for infringement of the design right, there must have been an intentional decision to infringe the owner's rights. Under the registration scheme, such intention need not be proved and damages may be awarded in cases of unintentional breach.

To qualify for the right to register the design it:

* must be a new design; and
* must have characteristics that give its appearance an original look.

This form of protection is often limited to the exterior of a product (rather than how it actually works—see section entitled 'Patents').

Due to the protection through the registered design right, its registration, and the confirmation that the IP belongs to the owner, selling or the licensed use of the design is more successful than with unregistered designs.

Changes introduced in the IPA 2014

* The ownership of design—**ss 2 and 6** provide that for designs created on or after 1 October 2014 or which are the subject of contracts after this date, the owner of a commissioned design will be the designer, not the person who commissioned the work unless the contract provides otherwise.

* Prior use—in the event that a person uses a design in good faith (eg the design was not copied) which is subsequently registered by another person, protection will be available to them against infringement actions (s 7).

* Criminal offence—prior to the **IPA 2014** the intentional copying of a registered design was a civil offence. The **2014 Act** now makes such action a criminal offence—based on the individual's intentional copying of the design without the consent of the owner and whilst knowing, or having reasonable belief, that the design was registered. A fine and/ or imprisonment of up to 10 years is available (s 13).

* Unregistered design right—the **IPA 2014** has simplified the process of a person qualifying for an unregistered design right in the UK.

Trade marks

Trade marks exist to distinguish between goods/services, and hence are a very valuable asset for businesses.

A trade mark is defined under the **Trade Marks Act (TMA) 1994 s 1(1)** as:

> any sign capable of being represented graphically which is capable of distinguishing goods or services of one undertaking from those of other undertakings. A trade mark may, in particular, consist of words (including personal names), designs, letters, numerals or the shape of goods or their packaging.

A trade mark (denoted by the ® symbol) identifies that the owner of the trade mark has registered it, and it prevents others from using the same image. A trade mark may be applied to a name or logo that identifies a product or service, or it could further include a slogan used by a brand or even some sound.

Following registration, the trade mark provides the owner with exclusive use of the mark, and those who infringe the mark are subject to a civil action by the owner, but it also enables the police and/or Trading Standards to initiate criminal proceedings for breach (eg with counterfeiters).

Infringement is committed where the trade mark and the other item:

- are identical; or
- are confusingly similar to make the consumer, for instance, buy one good believing it to belong to the trade mark holder; or
- do not use identical signs, but the trade mark has a reputation in the UK and its use takes advantage of, or is detrimental to, the distinctive character or the repute of the trade mark (s **10(1), (2), and (3)**).

The key issue regarding infringement of a trade mark is whether the consumer would believe there was a link between the proprietor and the goods being sold.

Refusal to grant a trade mark

The **TMA 1994 s 3** defines situations where an absolute refusal of registration will take place.

Enforcement

There exists an automatic right to enforce the trade mark against a person infringing the owner's rights and the courts are empowered, as with the common law, to award damages and grant injunctions. Where the trade mark breach has involved a criminal offence (eg dealing in counterfeit goods), beyond the loss to the owner where a common law remedy is available, Trading Standards may initiate an action that could lead to imprisonment for a period of 10 years and/or an unlimited fine.

A registered trade mark must be renewed every 10 years to remain effective (and may be renewed indefinitely), and where the owner has not registered it, the action to ensure protection against unauthorized use lies in the common law through the tort 'passing-off'.

> ### *Irvine v Talksport* [2003]
>
> The defendants had used a distorted, but still recognizable image of Eddie Irvine (a famous F1 racing driver) to endorse their product. This led to his claim for damages for the tortious act of 'passing off.' Irvine had a property right in his goodwill which could be protected from unlicensed use comprising of false claims of association or endorsement of a third party's business or goods. Irvine's claim of passing off succeeded.

A registered trade mark is enforceable throughout the UK whereas unregistered marks may not be applicable to such an extent and may be confined to enforcement in restricted geographical areas.

Patents

A business may seek to protect an invention, such as a new (non-obvious) product, or through a new way of making the product (a new process) that has an industrial application and has not been excluded from patentability (exclusions are identified in the **Patents Act (PA) 1977** ss 1 and 4A). An invention would constitute an inventive step where it would not have been obvious to someone with skill and experience in the area.

To be considered as new, the invention must not form part of the **state of prior art**—it must be a 'novelty' (this includes all factors that were publicly available prior to the invention). 'State of prior art' means that the invention must not have been made available to the public in the world, in any way, before the 'priority date' (s 2).

Revision tip

A patent need not relate to a completely new item but, rather, it could include a new way in which an item already in existence is produced (eg the bag-less vacuum cleaner developed by the Dyson company—*Dyson Appliances Ltd v Hoover Ltd* [2001]).

PA 1977 s 1(1) provides that a patent may be granted if the following criteria are satisfied:

- that the invention to be patented is new;
- that there is an inventive step involved (not obvious to a person with knowledge and experience in the area);
- that it is capable of industrial application (as such it is capable of being made or used); and
- that the granting of the patent is not to be excluded by the PA 1977 s 1(2), 1(3), or 4A.

Section 1(2), (3), and 4A outline which features will not satisfy the requirements of 'inventions' and hence are incapable of patents being applied.

Exploitation

The power of a patent is that it provides the owner with a monopoly right to exploit (work, sell on, or license) in a specific territory and for up to a 20-year period, even where another person, acting independently of the owner of the patent, could have developed the same invention.

Inventive step

The necessity of an inventive step (as defined in s 3) prevents a monopoly being created over things generally known by a person skilled in the art. *Pozzoli SpA v BDMO SA* [2007] identified the four steps to be applied in assessing the existence of an inventive step:

- identify the notional person skilled in the art and their relevant common knowledge;
- identify the inventive step/concept in question (or if this is not possible then it should be construed);
- identify differences between the matter in question and the invention patented; and
- consider whether the differences present constitute obvious steps or those which would require invention.

Infringement

Infringement occurs where the patented item/process is exploited in the UK without consent. However, a breach/infringement of the patent will not occur where the 'breach' is performed for research/experimentation (s 60(5)(b)), or where its use is for private rather than commercial purposes (s 60(5)(a)). Infringement of a patent is determined on a decision as to whether or not a very similar product comes within the scope of the exclusive right—see *Catnic Components Ltd v Hill & Sons Ltd* [1982].

Revision tip

Note the uncertainty, and possible unfairness to third parties, of this purposive method of interpretation. However, a literal interpretation could make the patent worthless for the right-holder.

Situations where a person infringes a patent in force in the UK are included in s 60(1).

The IPA 2014 has extended the grounds on which the UK-IPO can provide an invalidity opinion on patents and the Comptroller has been empowered with the ability to revoke a patent for obviousness. This is no longer restricted to actions based on earlier filed applications but applies to all grounds of lack of novelty.

Defences and remedies

Various defences to an action for infringement exist and these are considered in s 60(5)(a)–(f). Having established infringement, the remedies available are:

- injunction;
- damages;
- delivery up of any of the patented products;
- to account for any profits derived from their breach; and
- a declaration that the patent is valid and had been infringed through the defendant's actions.

Claims of a product/process as a patent, where no such patent has been granted, constitute a criminal offence.

A unitary patent

Patent protection, at present, requires inventors to maintain individual patents in each country where they do business and these are regulated in the national courts of each country. The European Patents Office can examine and grant patents for 38 States in Europe under the **European Patent Convention**, and once created, they are treated as national patents (called European bundle patents). However, these are subject to national rules and procedures and are required to be renewed individually in each State. This causes significant costs, bureaucracy, and difficulties in enforcement due to the lack of a single system for EU patent protection. The EU has sought to reduce these problems through enactment of two Regulations (the most immediately significant is **Regulation (EU) No 1257/2012** of The European Parliament and of the Council of 17 December 2012 implementing enhanced cooperation in the area of the creation of unitary patent protection) which will enable parties to challenge and defend unitary patents in a single court system—known as the Unified Patent Court. A unitary patent will provide uniform protection among the signatory Member States; it will have a single renewal fee system, and complements rather than replaces the current system of patents granted by the European Patents Office and national patents offices. As of 15 December 2015 the Select Committee which represents the EU Member States participating in the unitary patent formalized the necessary agreements into a complete secondary legal framework to give effect to the unitary patent system.

The Unified Patent Court

The UK signed an intergovernmental agreement in February 2013, along with the other EU Member States, for the creation of a Unified Patent Court (UPC) which is a specialist patents court common to the participating States. The UPC is comprised of a Court of First Instance and a Court of Appeal. Its primary purpose (specific rules for its procedures are in draft form and cannot be formalized in advance of the court being established) is to hear disputes regarding the validity and infringements of the new system of unitary patent.

Significantly, it will not have competence to hear matters regarding national patent rights (ie those relating to national patent offices).

To give effect to the UPC, a new s 88A was introduced into the PA 1977 enabling the Secretary of State to make the necessary order. A draft Statutory Instrument (SI), The Patents (Amendment) (EU Exit) Regulations 2018, has been laid before the UK Parliament which seeks to maintain this 'retained' EU law in the event of a no-deal Brexit. There is confusion as to this SI, given reference to powers held by the UK 'comptroller' and the UPC—despite the comptroller not being bound by the CJEU nor being able to make a reference to it (whilst the UPC is and can do so). However, clarification will be offered following the agreement ultimately reached between the UK and the EU as to the relationship between the two from 2019.

The Intellectual Property (Unjustified Threats) Act 2017

In a move to stop the development of 'patent trolls' who claim infringement of IP rights and initiate legal actions for damages, the 2017 Act was established. The Act was designed, in part at least, to restrict the time and expense of defending unmeritorious claims and to prevent the threats of legal actions against those who are (legitimately) exploiting IP rights.

The Act provides alleged IP infringers with a standalone right of action against an IP owner who threatens legal action, although a threat can be justified (the holder can prove the right subsists and is being infringed), which will constitute a defence. It applies to patents, trade marks, and registered and unregistered designs (although copyright and passing-off are not covered).

An actionable threat requires the following:

* A threat of infringement action is issued;
* A reasonable person, threatened with such action, would be aware that:
  1) the IP exists; and
  2) that the threat is to an infringement action to an act taking place, or would take place, in the UK;
* The person is aggrieved by the threat; and
* The threat is not in an excluded category and cannot be justified.

Damages, injunctions, and declaratory relief are the remedies available.

The General Data Protection Regulation ((EU) 2016/679)

The General Data Protection Regulation (GDPR) was established to strengthen the EU data protection framework in relation to, for example, consent and the rights of data subjects, the transfer of data and security and data breaches, and consequences for non-compliance.

The General Data Protection Regulation ((EU) 2016/679)
****

It aimed to harmonize protection throughout the EU. It applies to data within and between EU Member States although individuals who consent may allow data processors to transfer the data beyond the EU/European Economic Area.

It was established due to the rapid technological changes occurring since the implementation of the **Data Protection Directive (95/46/EC)** (which the **GDPR** repealed) into national law. Member States were allowed to make changes (in limited circumstances) in the transposition of the **GDPR** and the UK achieved this through the **Data Protection Act (DPA) 2018**. The **GDPR** became directly applicable across the EU on 25 May 2018 and the **DPA 2018** came into force on 25 May 2018.

The **GDPR** provides some new data subject rights—such as the right to erasure/right to be forgotten—and has enhanced other rights—such as the right to be informed.

What is protected?

The **GDPR** protects the 'personal data' of a 'data subject'.

- Personal data includes:
  - Personal information (eg name and address);
  - Employment information;
  - Contracts (eg goods purchased by the data subject);
  - Health-related information.
- Data subject:
  - This is an identified/identifiable natural person who 'can be identified, directly or indirectly, in particular by reference to an identifier such as a name, an identification number, location data, an online identifier or to one or more factors specific to the physical, physiological, genetic, mental, economic, cultural or social identity of that natural person' (**Art 4(1), GDPR**).
  - The **DPA 2018** defines such a person as an 'identifiable living individual' (**s 3(3), Part 1**).

The data subject must *consent* to the processing of their data (**Art 6(1)(a)**).

Rights

Under the **GDPR** individuals have:

- The right to erasure (**Art 17**)
- The right to be informed
- The right of access (**Art 15**)
- The right to rectification (**Art 16**)
- The right to restrict processing (**Art 18**)

- The right to data portability (**Art 20**)
- The right to object to processing (**Art 21**)
- Rights in relation to automate decision making and profiling
  - The right to erasure—this enables individuals to request that data held about them be erased (subject to exceptions). Businesses are obliged to remove this data within one month of notification of the request.

Revision tip

How do businesses store data on their customers, in which areas or departments and on which systems? These will have to be addressed and categorized to ensure compliance with the **GDPR**. Be prepared to address how you might advise a business on complying with both the **GDPR** and the **DPA 2018**.

- The right to be informed—Businesses and other organizations must ensure individuals understand who is collecting their data and which data controllers are processing it. This is achieved by maintaining privacy policies and it is the controller business' responsibility to demonstrate their compliance with the **GDPR**.

Data Protection Officer

Businesses, such as a public authority which carries out large-scale systematic monitoring of individuals, are required to appoint a Data Protection Officer who will help with meeting the requirements of the **GDPR**, including monitoring compliance.

Data Controllers

This is a person who determines the purposes and means of processing personal data.

Data Processors

Data processors have responsibility for the implementation of measures for securing personal data during its processing activities. The legal responsibilities of the data processors may exceed the contractual responsibilities between the individual and the employer/business.

Thus, a marketing company may be both a data processor (they will collect personal information from a website visitor and those who complete online forms) and a data controller (they control that data, adapt it, combine it, and determine if they will keep the data and how it will be used).

GDPR and Brexit

Regardless of whether the UK withdraws from the EU, remains or establishes a new agreement with the EU the UK government has confirmed that the **GDPR** will continue (although it may be subject to some modification as necessary).

The Law Enforcement Directive 2016/6801

The **Law Enforcement Directive (LED**—in force since 5 May 2016) supplements the **GDPR** but the **GDPR** does not apply to those activities covered by the **LED**. This includes processing for national security purposes and processing of data for personal activities. Unlike the **GDPR**, the **LED** is not a directly applicable EU law. **Part 3 of the DPA 2018** transposes the **LED** into national law.

The Data Protection Act 2018

The **DPA 2018** is divided into 7 Parts, of which the following should be noted:

- **Part 2, Chapter 1** covers general processing, scope, and definitions in relation to **Part 2**.
- **Part 2, Chapter 2** supplements the **GDPR** and applies to data processing coming within the scope of the **GDPR**. Further, it identifies the restrictions and exemptions from the rules of the **GDPR** (similar to ss 29–35 of the **DPA 1988**).
- **Part 2, Chapter 3** explains how certain types of processing (to which the **GDPR** does not apply) will be regulated.
- **Part 3** identifies the processing of personal data by competent authorities for law enforcement purposes. It explains the implementation of the **LED**.
- **Part 5** explains the role and responsibilities of the Information Commissioner's Office.
- **Part 6** relates to data protection enforcement.

The **DPA 2018** provides an effective framework, transposing as it does the **GDPR**, for the UK's withdrawal from the EU as planned in 2019. Ensuring the equivalent standards as required under EU legislation will facilitate a continuation of data processing and transfers between the organizations in the UK and EU Member States.

Given the distinct features of both the **GDPR** and **DPA 2018**, it is important that businesses and those staff with responsibilities for data are familiar with the provisions of each.

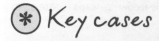 **Key cases**

Case	Facts	Principle
Arsenal Football Club Plc v Reed [2003] EWCA Civ 96	The professional football club had registered the club's names and the design of its badge. Reed had been selling goods with the name of the club and its emblem, but with the disclaimer that they were not official club merchandise.	The key issue regarding infringement of a trade mark is whether the consumer would believe there was a link between the proprietor and the goods being sold. The CJEU later held that the disclaimer was insufficient to prevent consumers making the link between the goods and the proprietor.
Catnic Components Ltd v Hill & Sons Ltd [1982] RPC 183	The claimant possessed a patent for a lintel. It provided that the rear face was vertical and the defendant relied on this description by making their lintel with a face with a 6-degree slant. The House of Lords held that a purposive rather than literal approach should be given to interpreting when an infringement occurs.	The traditional, certain, literal approach of interpretation may assist the courts, parties, and third parties, but may enable deviation and hence evasion of infringement. A method with more 'common sense' is to adopt a purposive approach, but this leads to uncertainty and provides the patentee with greater protection than envisaged when filing the patent.
Interlego AG v Tyco Industries Inc [1989] 1 AC 217	Tyco produced Lego bricks which had been subject to a previous patent and registered as a design, although the registration had expired. Tyco had made changes to the bricks, which were considered significant but failed in an attempt to copyright the new bricks.	Copyright is granted on original works, and this ruling prevented relatively minor modifications being granted a new copyright (essentially enabling the indefinite extension of copyright).
Re Harris' Patent [1985] RPC 19	An employee (a salesman) made a patentable invention. He had no requirement or expectation to invent and hence the invention belonged to him, not the employer.	An employer will generally be the owner of IP rights established by employees, unless the invention has no relation to their employment.

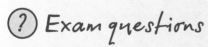 **Exam questions**

Problem question

Heberto owns premises in Sheffield, located on a popular road consisting of eating establishments and boutique clothes shops. From these premises he operates a coffee house (with the trading name 'Caffe di Napoli'). Heberto has recently attended a trade seminar at which he learns that trade marks apply to many more business signs than simply names and logos (as he previously assumed).

Exam questions

✳✳✳✳✳✳✳✳✳✳

On his return to Sheffield, Heberto makes an application to have the following words registered as a trade mark:

1. The name 'Caffe di Napoli';

2. The smell 'Of strong, freshly ground and roasted coffee'; and

3. The slogan 'Tantalizing tasty Tazo tea'.

Advise Heberto as to whether he will face difficulties regarding these applications.

An outline answer is included at the end of the book.

Essay question

Individuals who, whilst in the course of their employment, create inventions patented by their employers, were granted the right to be compensated (Patents Act 1977). However, in practice, this right was rarely successful.

With specific reference to appropriate case law, discuss whether this statement remains correct.

 Online Resources

To see an outline answer to this question visit www.oup.com/lawrevision/

Exam essentials

Exam topics

The first issue to consider when you're taking an examination in business law, as 'business law' can be a very broad, all-encompassing term, is to ensure you are aware of the module descriptor/content used at your institution. Business law may be a module providing exemptions from the various professional accounting bodies such as the ACCA and CIMA. It will therefore contain the full range of law topics (English legal system, European Union law, contract, torts, employment, and company law). Further, a business law module may focus primarily on company law, or it could concentrate on contract and consumer law. Therefore it is essential that you identify the scope of your module and know on which topics you should focus revision.

Types of exam question

Examinations may include a multiple-choice question format, and samples are included on the accompanying Online Resource Centre for your practice. However, the substantive examination questions fall into two broad categories: problem-type questions and essay-type questions:

- A problem-type question involves a hypothetical real-world scenario where parties will be involved in some legal issue/dispute which requires you to provide advice.
- An essay-type question will usually consist of a statement of law or policy which requires you to provide some form of critical commentary or analysis.

It is important to recognize that a problem-type question will involve the (critical) application of the law, whilst an essay-type question will require much more critical commentary/analysis, to provide a full and complete answer. I would certainly advise you to prepare for both as most examination questions involve a mixture of the two.

Structuring an answer

Having read through the exam paper (and read each question at least twice), you must first identify the topics being examined. You will be asked a specific question on each discrete examination topic—you will not be asked a question about 'contract law', but rather a specific aspect of contract law (validity of an agreement, consequences following breach, etc). Identifying what area of law is being examined and which key concepts and cases are significant will ensure your answer will be focused and accurate, whilst avoiding major omissions.

Exam essentials

****

Having identified the question and its scope, the next stage is to structure and plan your answer:

- The first stage is to describe the appropriate law.
- The second stage is to apply that law to the details outlined in the question.
- The third stage (and perhaps the most important to obtaining the higher grades) is your critical application/analysis of the law in relation to the facts of the question.

The answer should reference the statute or common law authority to ground your arguments and, possibly, incorporate academic commentary. It is the level and scope of detailed descriptive analysis, and the sophistication of critical application, that will determine the mark awarded.

Content of the answer

Make sure when you answer your question that you use the most up-to-date materials available. This means looking to newspaper reports, journal articles, academic and government reports, and reputable websites such as those included in the Online Resource Centre. By referencing such contemporary materials you will be demonstrating to the examiner your awareness of the interaction between academic and practical sources impacting on business law, but also recognizing that the law is dynamic and develops very quickly. You will also have incorporated demonstrable evidence of wider reading informing your answer. Remember, the first 40 per cent of marks are relatively easy to obtain (the identification and descriptive element), whilst the marks at the higher end generally comprise the critical analysis and application.

Discrete examinable topics

'Discrete' refers to a particular jurisdiction of law—for example, contract, company, torts. Most of the questions you will face in an examination will be based on one of these specific issues. However, remember that a particular scenario presented in an examination question could involve a number of legal areas. A constructive unfair dismissal, for example, would relate to that jurisdiction of employment law, but it may also involve a discriminatory aspect, a breach of contract, and even a criminal offence. Therefore, the legal implications of a problem question could involve numerous aspects of the law, so be prepared to discuss these and make sure you read the question carefully. It will explain on which areas of law to focus (and possibly in which to restrict) your answer.

Finally

Due to the breadth of legal topics included in business law, it would be impracticable for us to identify specific areas on which to focus your revision. Follow these approaches, having first read through your text-books and practised answering the questions contained within; use the indicative content answers available to gauge your understanding, ensure you attend lectures, and participate fully in seminars/tutorials/workshops and you should be in a strong position to approach your assessments with confidence.

Outline answers

Chapter 1

Problem answer

- This situation requires an awareness of where the threat of litigation may be helpful but also where it may not, for example a loss of future business; how will other customers be likely to react to AEL gaining a reputation as a company willing to resort to law; how big a problem is the issue; can the matter be resolved by ADR and, if so, which one, how would it be set up, etc, and what could be expected from it.

- A breach of contract claim may be brought against BigByte, but this could result in the relationship being terminated and costing AEL more in future sales and business than would a less adversarial system—hence ADR should be considered.

- There are many approaches to ADR including internal dispute resolution techniques, negotiations, the ombudsman scheme, and so on.

- The process for using ADR will begin with some form of negotiation; then, unless there is an arbitration agreement in the contract (as is often included in construction cases), the parties may attempt some form of mediation, and then possibly move towards conciliation and then arbitration in the event that the dispute cannot be resolved.

- The most common forms of ADR include Arbitration, Conciliation, and Mediation. Identify the advantages and disadvantages of each before explaining and justifying the choice provided in your answer.

- It may be useful to explain that, whilst cheaper than court action, where ADR fails it may lead to a court case being pursued—hence the advantages of ADR are lost.

Chapter 2

Problem answer

- The question involves discussion of variation of contract. It is important to recognize that the variation, like other promises, must be supported by consideration—hence the appropriate and, sometimes, conflicting case law in the area must be included.

- Identify the main rules of 'good' consideration—it must be sufficient (not adequate); it must not be past (as in *Re McArdle, Decd*); but the main element of the question is the next rule—existing duties are not good consideration.

- If the promisor is merely receiving what they are already entitled to, then there is no consideration furnished—*Collins v Godefroy*. Consider *Hartley v Ponsonby* in comparison with *Stilk v Myrick*; where the promisee exceeds their existing duty this can establish good consideration.

- Clearly, existing duties can amount to good consideration where a benefit is received and/or a detriment is avoided (and no unfair pressure or duress was used in the renegotiation)—*Williams v Roffey Bros & Nicholls (Contractors) Ltd*. Here Gordon is keeping his job (that would otherwise be lost on the winding-up of the employer's business) and this may amount to a benefit. Further, it does not appear that any unlawful pressure was applied to make Gordon agree to the offer.

- The answer could also offer the doctrine of promissory estoppel if *Williams v Roffey* does not apply. Estoppel is an equitable defence which stops a party that has made a (gratuitous) promise from reneging (*Central London Property Trust v High Trees House Ltd*). Hence, if Gordon wishes to claim the previous wages he agreed not to take, then Fred may attempt to defend such a claim using *High Trees* as precedent. However, now the economic problems have diminished, Gordon may be successful, using *High Trees*, to claim his previous wage structure from 2017.

Chapter 3

Problem answer

- Cal states that the dog has a pleasant demeanour (but fails to disclose the change of personality when in contact with balloons). Is this a term or representation? The case law must be used (as is identified in the answer to the essay question in this chapter) and as this is a statement of opinion rather than fact, it is likely to be held as a representation. Remember to apply the tests in determining a misrepresentation:

- a statement of material fact (not opinion) that induces the other party into the contract (*Bisset v Wilkinson*);
- a false representation (*Thomson v Christie Manson & Woods Ltd*);
- the innocent party believed the statement to be true (*Redgrave v Hurd*); and
- the representation induced the party into the contract (hence sufficiently important and materially relevant—*Edgington v Fitzmaurice*).

• The statement that the dog is a pure breed may be a term based on the documentation available to Cal, but there may also be a misrepresentation here—remember to consider the implications of it being an innocent misrepresentation and the effects that this would have for Malik in gaining a remedy.

• Therefore, this may involve a misrepresentation—is it actionable? Probably (although the tests would have to be applied) but it is vital to identify which, if any, form of misrepresentation it is as this will affect the remedies that are available.

• There may be an action for damages/rescission.

• Consider whether the statement is actionable under **Misrepresentation Act 1967 s 2(1)** and, if so, note the shifting burden of proof and the remedy of damages (*Royscot v Rogerson*).

Chapter 4

Problem answer

NB: The significance of the date of the events is important. If the purchases occurred on or after 1 October 2015 the **Consumer Rights Act 2015** is applicable. However, prior to this **SOGA 1979** is the operative legislative instrument and given that, for instance, a television may be expected to remain functional for a period of six years (the satisfactory quality), **SOGA** is likely to remain a source of rights for a number of years to come.

• If answering using reference to both **SOGA 1979** and **CRA 2015**, identify that **SOGA 1979** implies ss 12–15 into business-to-consumer

contracts whilst **CRA 2015** guarantees such rights. This is an important distinction.

• Sarah has protection of **SOGA 1979** and **CRA 2015** as she is acting as a consumer and the other party is not (a high street shop).

Question 1

The issue involves protection through **SOGA 1979 s 14(3)/CRA 2015 s 10** 'goods must be reasonably fit for the buyer's specified purpose'. Sarah has no remedy because the pillow is fit for its purpose (*Grant v Australian Knitting Mills Ltd*)—unless Sarah has identified her allergy and relied on the description by the retailer—*Griffiths v Peter Conway*.

Question 2

If a sale of goods takes place through a sample of a larger consignment, the bulk of the consignment must correspond to the sample (in practical terms, this section is of most use to businesses). The goods should also be free from defects that would make their quality unsatisfactory and would not have been apparent on a reasonable inspection (*Godley v Perry*). *Godley* is a good example to be used here (and also make sure you include the negligence/damages action available) **SOGA 1979 s 15/CRA 2015 s 13**.

Question 3

SOGA 1979 s 14(2)/CRA 2015 s 9 incorporates a term requiring the goods to be of a satisfactory quality. Goods are of satisfactory quality if they meet the standard that a reasonable person would regard as satisfactory, taking account of any description of the goods, the price (if relevant), and all the other relevant circumstances.

Chapter 5

Problem answer

• The question involves remedies for loss of enjoyment. The traditional view of the courts when determining the level of damages applicable has been to ignore any injured feelings or loss of enjoyment suffered (*Addis v Gramophone*). This is due to the problems inherent in quantifying such damages and the potential of opening the floodgates for claimants.

• Exceptions to this rule have been developed in various cases (include a discussion of

Outline answers

****

Malik v Bank of Credit & Commerce International). In relation to the problem question, the facts are based on *Jarvis v Swans Tours*.

• In *Jarvis*, a solicitor booked a 15-day Christmas winter sports holiday with Swans Tours. The brochure described the venue—a 'house party centre'—in very attractive terms.

• The relevant facts were that only 13 people were at the venue in the first week and no other guests in the second week. No one at the resort could speak English; in the first week there were no full-length skis for Jarvis to use and in the second week the skis were available but the boots supplied were of no use; the live entertainment consisted of a yodeller from the locality, who sang four to five songs very quickly and then left; and the bar was only open on one evening.

• Jarvis sought to recover the cost of the holiday and his salary for the two weeks spent on holiday. The Court of Appeal held that Jarvis was entitled to be compensated for his disappointment and distress at the loss of entertainment and facilities that he had been promised in Swans Tours' brochure.

• Damages should recognize the nature of this type of contract, and as it was specifically for enjoyment, if the contract does not provide what was promised then damages could be extended to account for that.

Chapter 6

Problem answer

Task 1

The test establishing negligence liability will be outlined and described—duty of care, breach of duty, and consequential damage. Relevant case law will be included along with the case on which this question is based—*Sayers v Harlow BC*.

Task 2

This rule should be described and applied to the situation where the claimant has sustained an injury which affects her more than an 'average' person due to a pre-existing condition.

Task 3

This should be defined and explained as a partial defence—it will still enable the claimant to a proportion of damages. The better students will give specific examples of the percentage reductions (supported by appropriate case law), but the main issue is how Marala would be considered as contributing to her own misfortune. The student should also discuss whether Marala's attempt to climb out of the toilet cubicle was reasonable.

Task 4

The issue of whether Marala can claim for the lost holiday should allow discussion of the various cases such as *Hadley v Baxendale* and *Victoria Laundry*. The lack of foreseeability will be considered as the question asks for a discussion of remoteness.

Chapter 7

Problem answer

• In relation to Ahmed, the question is about discrimination on the ground of religion or belief. The **Equality Act 2010** makes it unlawful to discriminate against a person on the grounds of any religion, religious or philosophical belief, a lack of any religion, or a lack of any belief. Further, where it is perceived that an individual holds a religion or belief and suffers discrimination on this basis, or they suffer discrimination because of association with another who holds the religion or belief, an unlawful act is committed.

• A defence available to claims of direct discrimination is that a specific religion or belief is an occupational qualification (OQ). In Ahmed's case, where an organization has a specific ethos based on a religion or belief, such as religious organizations, the need for persons of a specific religion or belief may be justified. This is not applicable to all jobs that the organization has to fill, and the employer will have to demonstrate that the OQ is reasonable and proportionate in the circumstances.

• In relation to Susan, consider the issue of reasonable belief and 'relevant failures' in the **ERA 1996 s 43B**. Further, the **Equality Act** offers protection to a person who has been victimized because they have made a complaint/allegation in relation to a complaint of discrimination.

• Mark's situation involves discrimination on the basis of sexual orientation and 'homophobic banter'. Consider the protection available in the Equality Act and *English v Thomas Sanderson Ltd.*

Chapter 8

Problem answer

• The situation involves dismissal. It should be established whether Helen has made the employees aware of the policy about security of company information—is it in the employees' contracts, works' handbook, an oral announcement, etc?

• Identify if the employees qualify for protection under the **ERA 1996**.

• Outline the potentially fair reasons to dismiss an employee (**ERA 1996 s 98**).

• In cases of dismissal, the employer should carry out as much investigation as possible to identify if the employees were involved in the misconduct.

• The employees involved are the only ones that could reasonably have accessed the information and the employer may wish to dismiss them for the potentially fair reason of (mis)conduct (**ERA 1996 s 98**). The employer does not require proof—just reasonable grounds on which to hold/maintain belief of misconduct (*British Home Stores v Burchell*).

• Where a group of workers are involved in a misconduct, and it is reasonable for the employer to assume they were all involved, yet following an investigation identification of the actual perpetrator(s) cannot be achieved, all of the group may be dismissed (*Parr v Whitbread*).

• Selective dismissals may be justified where the employer possesses solid and sensible grounds for retaining one of the employees.

• Emma is employed on a fixed-term contract. She would be entitled to the balance of the contract if she claimed wrongful, rather than unfair, dismissal. However, note the problem here with after-discovered reasons which would be allowed to make an otherwise wrongful dismissal a lawful dismissal, but will not stop an unfair dismissal being unfair. After-discovered reasons may reduce any compensation payable in cases of unfair dismissal (if Emma did give Jack the password). Therefore, Helen should continue her investigations into the unauthorized access to the computer.

Chapter 9

Problem answer

• As a sole trader, Czarina has complete control over her business; she has substantial risks if she continues to operate as a sole trader but expands the business (and the business fails). The key element here is Czarina's unlimited liability.

• Czarina could form a simple partnership with someone else who has money to invest (put into the partnership) or who may offer skills/customers, etc that would make the expansion of the business (potentially) more secure. The issues of joint and several liability, good faith, and the right for management of the business should be raised as possible areas for concern. Also Czarina and her partner(s) would share any losses, but they would also share profits and the issue of unlimited liability remains.

• Czarina could establish a limited company. Issues of separate legal personality (*Salomon v Salomon*) should be raised and the main advantage of limited liability of the shareholders should be specifically explained. This may be a key advantage when Czarina is attempting to expand her business. Further, benefits such as perpetual succession of the company and the (apparent) ease of obtaining credit (when compared to sole traders) should be discussed.

• A disadvantage to be explained is the increased external regulation that limited companies must comply with (compared with sole traders). This will add additional administrative burdens and require disclosure of information that the other, simpler, forms of business organization do not have to contend with.

• Finally, sum up the arguments and draw a conclusion as to which form of business would be most beneficial to Czarina (it is your choice and should be acceptable insofar as it is supported by your arguments).

Chapter 10

Problem answer

The **CA 2006** identifies duties imposed on directors. They are to be interpreted and applied in the same way as the common law rules and equitable principles on which they were based.

Outline answers

✳✳✳✳✳✳✳✳✳✳✳✳

General duties relevant to the question include:

- duty to act within their powers;
- duty to promote the success of the company;
- duty to exercise independent judgement;
- duty to exercise reasonable care, skill, and diligence;
- duty to avoid conflicts of interest.

Specifically in relation to Jubril, the following duty is most relevant:

- A director of a company is not allowed to accept a benefit from a third party that is due to them being a director of the company and their acts or omissions as a director. Note that the duty is not infringed where the acceptance of a benefit 'cannot reasonably be regarded as likely to give rise to a conflict of interest'.

- Important questions to be raised are whether the value of the gift, its nature, or frequency has influenced the director's decision-making. Or perhaps the court will focus on the proximity between the providing of the gift and the conclusion of the action or omission in determining whether a breach of CA 2006 s 176 has occurred.

- This duty is concerned with benefits such as bribes (in cash or in kind) that will impact on the impartiality of the director in acting for the company. Where a benefit is provided to the director and not the company, the director's objectivity may be compromised. The Act requires the director to consult the company's constitution to determine which actions are acceptable, and which are not. Transparency of any gifts provided and how decisions were made may ensure the director does not transgress their obligations in this area.

- The director as agent of the company and holding of a secret commission/bribe on trust for the company (principal) could be discussed.

Chapter 11

Problem answer

- The definition of a trade mark (provided in the TMA 1994 s 1(1)) should be highlighted, and that where it is denoted by the ® symbol it identifies that the owner of the trade mark has registered it, and it prevents others from using the same image.

- A trade mark may be applied to a name or logo that identifies a product or service, or it could further include a slogan used by a brand or even some sound (*Shield Mark BV v Joost Kist hodn Memex*).

- Following registration, the trade mark provides the owner with exclusive use of the mark, and those who infringe the mark are subject to a civil action by the owner.

- The TMA 1994 s 3 defines where an absolute refusal of registration will take place—these instances should be listed and applied as relevant.

- A registered trade mark is enforceable throughout the UK whereas unregistered marks may not be applicable to such an extent and may be confined to enforcement in restricted geographical areas.

- Prior use of the marks may impact on the registration process so consultation with the UK-IPO is advised.

- A slogan may function as a trade mark: *Have a Break TM* in relation to Kit Kat chocolate bars and *I Can't Believe It's Yoghurt* as a slogan were applied to goods. In relation to the question, the slogan has already been registered by the Starbucks Coffee Company.

- Smells can function as trade marks insofar as they satisfy the requirement of distinctiveness (although difficulty arises in relation to smells as an olfactory sign).

Glossary

Agent   A person who has the authority to act on behalf of another (the principal), and will bind the principal in contracts as if the principal had personally made the agreement.

Breach of contract   When a party fails to complete his/her obligations under the contract, he/she may be in breach, allowing the injured party to seek a remedy.

Breach of statutory duty   A statute may impose a duty but fail to mention any civil law sanctions. In order to claim under the statute, the claimant must demonstrate that Parliament intended liability in tort to follow from the breach.

Business efficacy   This expression has been used when describing how the courts may imply terms in order to produce an intended or anticipated result in the contract.

Common law   Law created through judicial decisions. It is a body of law that was being developed before a united system of government had been formed in England.

Consensus ad idem   This is the Latin term for an 'agreement as to the same thing' in English law or more commonly referred to as a 'meeting of minds' between the parties.

Consideration   Simple contracts have to be a bargain rather than a gratuitous promise (that cannot be enforced). Consideration is something of value that makes the agreement a bargain (the price you pay for a promise).

Constitution   The constitution is a system defining the power of the State/State bodies, and regulating their actions, thereby ensuring accountability.

Contra proferentem   This is a rule whereby the courts, generally, will interpret an exclusion clause narrowly and against the party that is seeking to rely on it.

Corporation   A legal entity, such as a company, that possesses its own legal personality separate from the members.

Debenture   Written evidence of a secured loan given by the lender to the company. It has been described as a document which either creates a debt or acknowledges it.

Delegated legislation   Laws that enable an individual/body to pass legislation under the authority and control of Parliament. These include Statutory Instruments, Orders in Council, and by-laws.

Direct effect   Legislation from the EU creates rights for individuals in the Member States. Direct effect of the law requires a domestic court to apply the EU law, even in the absence of national implementing legislation.

Dividend   The distributable profits of a company to shareholders.

Duress   Compelling a party to enter a contract on the basis of a threat. If sufficient, it will make the contract voidable.

Employee   An individual who works under a 'contract *of service*'.

Equitable remedy   Discretionary remedies granted by the courts, generally where damages would not provide an adequate remedy. Examples of equitable remedies include injunctions, rescission, and specific performance.

Expectation damages   Identifies what the injured party would have achieved from the successful completion of the contract, and seeks to place him/her, as far as money can, in that position.

Fiduciary duty   A fiduciary has authority belonging to another person/body, and he/she is obliged to exercise this for the other party's benefit. An example of a relationship establishing fiduciary duties is between a solicitor and his/her client.

Force majeure clauses   This is an element of frustration in determining how to deal with events that are beyond the control of the parties (wars, acts of God, and so on).

Frustration   An event that is neither party's fault, may render the contract impossible to perform, or is radically different from that agreed. This leads to the contract being frustrated (cannot

Glossary

continue) and results in the parties being discharged from further responsibilities.

Independent contractor An individual who works under a 'contract *for services*'. He/she has the ability (and option) to work for several employers, and enjoy better tax benefits, but lacks many elements of employment protection that employees enjoy.

Injunction There are two main types of injunction—mandatory injunctions and prohibitory injunctions (although interim injunctions may be granted prior to a full hearing to prevent injury to the claimant). Failing to follow the order of an injunction will result in the transgressor being guilty of contempt of court.

Intention to create legal relations A legally enforceable contract must be one where the parties understand and accept that failure to fulfil obligations under the agreement may result in legal consequences.

Inter alia The Latin phrase meaning 'among other things'. This may be used, for example, to denote where other things were said in a ruling by a court, beyond the point being reported.

Judiciary The body of the judges that interpret and apply the law. The 'judiciary' often refers to the senior judges in the Supreme Court, Court of Appeal, and the judicial wing of the Privy Council.

Legal personality The rights attached to a natural person and/or an artificial thing, such as a corporation.

Legislation Law created through, or under the authority of, Parliament. It is the highest form of law and is not subject to challenge by the courts.

Liquidated damages These are damages that are determined in the contract in advance of a breach. They must be a pre-estimate of loss and not a penalty clause.

Mitigation In the event of a breach of contract, the injured party has an obligation to limit his/her losses as far as is reasonably possible/practical.

Mutuality of obligations There is an obligation for an employee to offer his/her services to the employer (attend work) and there is a mutual obligation for the employer to provide work/pay. This is an essential component of 'employee' status.

Nudum pactum This is a promise made with no consideration to support it.

Nuisance This is an unlawful interference that prevents an owner/occupier's enjoyment of his/her land.

Obiter dicta These are statements made by judges that are not part of the *ratio*, and hence are not part of the judgment of the case. They are not binding on lower courts but they are of persuasive authority and may be followed in future cases where the issue is raised.

Offeree The party(s) to whom an offer has been made.

Offeror The party making an offer and setting out the terms by which he/she is willing to be bound.

Pari passu An interpretation from the Latin means 'with equal step' and can be considered as meaning shares that rank without preference.

Parliament Parliament comprises the House of Commons and the House of Lords at Westminster, and also the monarch. All three institutions are involved in the legislative system, with Parliament scrutinizing the work of the government and holding it to account.

Penalty clause A clause which seeks to stop the other party from breaching the contract by imposing the threat of a penalty that is not a genuine pre-estimate of loss, and will be held void.

Precedent This is a system where the decisions of higher courts (through case law/common law) bind lower courts due to the hierarchical system of the court structure. Precedent is established from the *ratio decidendi* of the case.

Principal The person who instructs the agent to work on his/her behalf.

Promisee The party to whom a promise is made.

Promisor The party making the promise.

Promissory estoppel A doctrine providing an equitable defence preventing a party who has made a promise to vary a contract for the other party's benefit from later reneging on it and attempting to enforce the original contract.

Proximity The close relationship between the parties to a negligence action. It is an essential feature to establish a duty of care.

Pure economic loss This is where the claimant's losses are not connected with any physical loss or damage. This is typically in the case of negligent advice or information provided to the claimant.

Quantum meruit 'As much as he has earned' (an amount paid in relation to the work performed).

Ratio decidendi This is the part of the judicial decision that is binding on all lower courts. The judiciary explain the previous case law and establish the legal principle on which the case has been decided. The *ratio* is not identified as such, rather, it has to be 'found' through reading the judgment and identifying the salient factors leading to the decision.

Rectification This remedy enables a written document (eg a contract) to be changed (eg including/removing clauses) more accurately to reflect the terms that were identified in the oral agreement subsequently reduced in writing.

Red-circle An employer who has conducted a job evaluation study to make pay structures transparent may protect the pay of a group of affected workers where they have been assessed, and they are to be downgraded.

Reliance damages Designed to prevent the injured party from suffering financial harm and placing him/her in the position in which he/she was before the contract had been established.

Representations Statements in the negotiations of a contract that do not amount to a term, but which may lead to a claim for misrepresentation if breached.

Repudiation To end or reject a contract, usually in response to a breach by the other party.

Rescind (rescission) Rescission is an equitable remedy and refers to a situation where the contract is set aside.

Restraint of trade clause This is a contractual clause that prevents or restricts an employee from competing with the employer for a specific duration and a specific region/area of industry.

Revocation An offer may be withdrawn (revoked) by the offeror before being accepted by the offeree.

Rogue A scoundrel/person with no ethics. A crook.

Separation of powers To ensure too much power is not vested in one body, and that a system of accountability through 'checks and balances' exists, the three elements of the State (the executive, the legislature, and the judiciary) must have clear demarcation between them. This ensures there is sufficient independence in these three branches of government.

Specific performance A remedy that is available when monetary damages are insufficient and do not adequately compensate the injured party for his/her loss. This is a court order compelling the party in breach to perform his/her contractual obligations.

State of prior art In patent law, an invention may be refused a patent because it is not novel. Therefore, if it can be demonstrated that 'prior art' existed before the patent applied for (through documents and other evidence) then the patent will not be granted.

Statute A statute refers to an act of the legislature. It may be referred to as an 'Act of Parliament' or 'legislation'.

Strict liability Liability is imposed due to the fact that the product contains a defect. There is no requirement to demonstrate negligence on the part of the defendant.

Summary dismissal This is an immediate dismissal (without any notice). Essentially, the employer has sacked the employee 'on the spot'.

Tortfeasor The party who has committed the tort.

Transposition EU Directives establish laws that the Member State must put into effect in its own legal system. Member States may choose the manner and form which this takes

Glossary

✱✱✱✱✱✱✱✱✱✱✱

but they must have an Act, Regulation, or administrative order in place to which individuals in the Member State will have access. (For example, the EU Working Time Directive was transposed into English law through the Working Time Regulations 1998.)

Unfair dismissal   A dismissal in breach of statutory requirements—the Employment Rights Act 1996. When considering unfair dismissal, always look at s 98 in relation to the reasonableness of the employer's decision to dismiss, and the procedural requirements established by ACAS.

Unliquidated damages   Damages that are incapable of being pre-determined and are calculated by the court.

Vicarious liability   Holding another party (usually an employer) responsible/liable for the actions of the tortfeasor.

Volenti non fit injuria   The Latin phrase relating to a voluntary assumption of risk where a person engages in an event and agrees to and accepts the inherent risks. If injured, he/she is prevented from bringing a claim.

Winding-up   This is the process of bringing a company to an end. As a corporation possesses its own separate legal personality, it must be formally wound up by a court to 'die'.

Written resolution   This is a mechanism for the board of directors to make a decision without having to meet in person. The resolution is valid and effective as if it has been agreed and passed at a meeting, if signed by all the directors entitled to receive notice of it.

Wrongful dismissal   A dismissal in breach of the contract of employment, most commonly seen when a worker is unjustifiably dismissed contrary to the required notice period.

Index

Index

✳✳✳✳✳✳✳✳✳✳✳✳

Index

✳✳✳✳✳✳✳✳✳✳✳✳✳

Index

****

Index

****

Index

Index

****